THE SEEKER

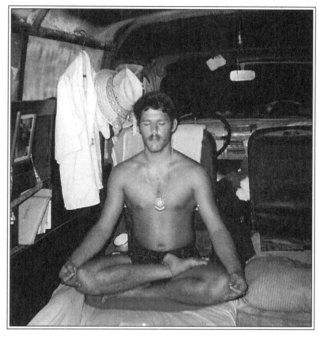

Marijuana,
self-realization,
meditation, self-hypnosis,
psychedelic drugs, yoga,
acid gurus...

Jeff Johnson's search
for the clear light

M. MACIEL AND J. JACQUART

The Seeker
Jeff Johnson's search for the clear light

Published by Calvary Chapel Publishing (CCP)
a resource ministry of Calvary Chapel Costa Mesa
3800 South Fairview Rd.
Santa Ana, CA 92704

First printing, 2003

All Scripture quotations in this book, unless otherwise indicated, are taken from the King James Version.

Library of Congress Control Number: 20022116205

ISBN: 1-931667-65-9
        (PBK)

Printed in the United States of America.

Cover Design: Mike Cox / Alpha Advertising

Back cover photo taken on Todos Santos Island, Mexico, on Jeff's 41st birthday. Photographer unknown.

Foreword

In what is perhaps the oldest book of literature, one of the main characters asks the question, "Where can I find God?" This ancient quest by man to find God has continued throughout the ages. Over three thousand years ago, King David cried out, "My soul thirsts for the living God."

To the present day, men and women will travel to distant lands and remote corners of the world in their search for God. Sadly, most are unsuccessful in their quest.

This book, however, recounts the story of one who searched for God and finally found Him. As a result, he has helped lead thousands of others in their pursuit to find and know God.

Chuck Smith
Pastor, Calvary Chapel Costa Mesa, California

Table of Contents

TABLE OF CONTENTS

Preface

During the late 1960s, Jeff Johnson was a surfing, opium-smoking hippie, following drug guru Timothy Leary, and living on the North Shore of the Hawaiian island of Oahu.

Caught in the turmoil of the '60s as an adolescent, he attempted to fill the inner void and restlessness he felt with drugs, sex, parties, and surfing.

Searching for the clear light—the truth—he studied under Paramahansa Yogananda, founder of the Self-Realization Fellowship. He also dabbled in various Eastern philosophies and practices, including: Buddhism, Hinduism, Hare Krishna, meditation, and yoga. His search even led him to try hypnosis as well as numerous types of illegal drugs.

In this "Age of Aquarius," this time of peace and love, Jeff's drug and alcohol use progressed from marijuana to barbiturates and amphetamines; LSD, peyote, and opium soon followed. What he wanted was to know truth. What he got was a drug habit that couldn't be satisfied, police arrests, broken relationships, a son given up for adoption, emptiness, and disillusionment.

Sensing that there must be something more to why we're here, he continued his search until he found the inner peace and sense of destiny he longed for, followed by success beyond his imagination. The truth found him. This is his amazing story.

Dedication

I want to thank my Lord and Savior, Jesus Christ, for hearing my cry—to God be the Glory!

> *Hear, O LORD, when I cry with my voice: have mercy also upon me, and answer me.*
>
> *When thou saidst, Seek ye my face; my heart said unto thee, Thy face, LORD, will I seek.*
>
> *Psalm 27:7-8*

In the very beginning of my search, after finding the truth, I was losing my home and family. God spoke to me through Matthew 6:33, "But seek ye first the kingdom of God, and his righteousness; and all these things shall be added unto you." I found, as I hope and pray you will find, peace for the seeker ... He is faithful! Wise men still seek Him!

This is dedicated to all who seek Him. All the glory goes to God!

1968

Mike, Paul, and Jeff on the North Shore of Oahu, 1968.

Chapter

1

Turn On, Tune In, Drop Out

In the lotus position, upside down, fingers touching to allow the energy flow, Jeff Johnson focused on attempting to look through his *third eye*.

"Om ..." he chanted.

Jeff was trying to encounter the primeval powers and forces to find a higher reality. He was studying the mystical teachings of Paramahansa Yogananda, founder of the Self-Realization Fellowship. Learning how to twist his body into extreme postures, meditate, and cleanse his system with natural foods, he diligently went through all the lessons. He wanted to become a modern shaman and follow the ancient path.

He participated in the psychic-altering practices promoted in *The Psychedelic Experience*, a book written by LSD guru Timothy Leary. Dropping acid every chance he got, Jeff was having some incredible trips. All this was part of his search for a higher reality, the *clear light*, trying to connect to *the other world* and attain *samadhi*, a totally serene state.

"Om ..." he repeated in loud monotones.

The phone rang, but Jeff tried to ignore it.

"Om ..." He increased his volume.

The ringing persisted. He sighed, slowly got to his feet, and answered the call.

"Jeff, man, I've got good news." It was his friend, Doug.

"What?" His tone reflected his irritation about being interrupted.

"I'm in Hawaii, and it's awesome. You've got to come over."

"Why?"

"You're not going to believe this place," Doug said. "God is over here, man. It's so peaceful. It's beautiful. It's the heaviest place you could live right now. You've got to come."

"Well, I can tell you God is not in LA," Jeff replied, still feeling a bit dizzy from being upside down.

"So what are you waiting for, man? Come on over. The surf's incredible. Bring your board."

Jeff hesitated for a moment, and then answered, "Why not? I'll be there."

Jeff was a high-energy guy who had tried many things, starting with alcohol at age thirteen, progressing to getting stoned and selling drugs, street fighting, stealing, serving jail time, participating in love-ins, and now getting involved in self-realization, hypnosis, and yoga. All of these things became empty and even boring to him after awhile. In fact, each new thing he tried lasted about six months before he moved on to something else.

During the '60s, America was experiencing enormous cultural upheaval. The '50s beatniks turned into the '60s hippies. It was a time when some were promoting love-ins and peace, while others led a youthful rebellion with their long hair, hallucinogenic drugs, and sudden fascination with Eastern mysticism. Rebellion, fueled by drugs, racism, and the Vietnam War, led to college riots and the burning of draft cards and American flags. Violence and change swept the nation.

At the beginning of the decade, President John Kennedy captured America with hopeful and challenging phrases like

"Ask not what your country can do for you—ask what you can do for your country." He promoted the Peace Corps and inspired youth to sign up by the thousands. But then came the humiliation of the Bay of Pigs and Fidel Castro's victory in Cuba, followed by Nikita Khrushchev, the Soviet leader, building the Berlin Wall, dividing East and West. In the third year of his presidency, John Kennedy, while motoring through Dallas, Texas, suddenly slumped in the seat of a blue Lincoln convertible, murdered by a single gunshot.

The Civil Rights movement endured the burning of Watts in Los Angeles and the race riots in Detroit, and then nearly collapsed with the murder of Martin Luther King, Jr. He spoke of his dream—a time when black and white children would form one tolerant and loving nation. Just five years later in 1968, a bullet took his life on a balcony in Memphis. Robert Kennedy also became the victim of an assassin's bullet. While NASA worked towards landing on the moon, America's icons were dying.

In the midst of this violence, the Age of Aquarius birthed a new generation of hippies talking of peace and love. They held their own festivals where they listened to rock and blues music. The girls wore flowers in their hair and long peasant dresses, or no clothes at all. The young men grew long hair and beards and wore bandanas. They drank beer and wine, smoked pot, got high, and had sexual orgies. Some began living in communes. The establishment generation fought against the counterculture over values and principles—the straights versus the druggies. Confused and disillusioned, many turned to psychedelic drugs hoping for a spiritual, psychic, and consciousness evolution.

Rock 'n' roll music lyrics were laced with drug themes. The Beatles sang "Lucy in the Sky with Diamonds" about LSD. Jimi Hendrix's "Purple Haze" was about marijuana; he pioneered heavy metal and reshaped rock 'n' roll when he lit his guitar on fire at the Monterey International Pop Music Festival. Mick Jagger and the Rolling Stones sang

15

"Street Fighting Man," The Doors sang "Light My Fire," and the Beach Boys sang "Little Deuce Coupe" and "California Girls." Bob Dylan sang "The Times They Are A-Changin'," warning about nuclear war. Others like Led Zeppelin, Janis Joplin, Big Brother & the Holding Company, The Supremes, The Temptations, Otis Redding, Stevie Wonder, Simon & Garfunkel, Jefferson Airplane, The Who, James Brown, and Aretha Franklin all made their mark in the '60s. The rock bands mesmerized their audiences with psychedelic light shows, smoke, and fire.

During all of this, Jeff expanded his personal drug use, progressing from marijuana to barbiturates and amphetamines to LSD. Although he was always looking for a bigger and better high and hoping to discover some truth, to find *the light*, nothing seemed to satisfy for very long. When his friend, Doug, called him from Hawaii, he was ready for another change—new highs and new experiences. Maybe Hawaii held the answers he was looking for.

He borrowed money from his mother and bought a plane ticket.

A Surfer's Paradise

Within a week of Doug's phone call, Jeff abandoned his drug dealing business in Southern California. He took his surfboard, packed some clothes in a gym bag, stuffed his books in a backpack, and headed for Oahu.

Flying over the Hawaiian Islands, a beautiful tropical landscape of lush vegetation was revealed. Oahu was a real paradise, known for its sky blue waters and for world-class surfing, beaches with powder white sand, orchid-studded jungles, cascading

Jeff just before he left for Hawaii, 1968.

waterfalls plunging into tranquil pools, and fields fringed by breadfruit trees and hibiscus. In awe of this spectacular and unspoiled display of nature, Jeff felt renewed already. However, after his five-hour flight, he was ready to drop some acid.

Doug met him at the airport. "*Aloha!*" He said, putting a fresh flower lei over Jeff's head. "Welcome to paradise."

"*Mahalo*," Jeff said, "Thank you."

They walked from the airport and started to hitchhike to the North Shore. Within a short time, someone pulled over in an old van, and Jeff tossed his board in the back. They drove past Waikiki Beach to check out the surf and headed for the interior of the island.

Doug explained their destination as *"Mauka,"* or up the mountain. As they climbed, they passed thick tropical foliage and beautiful flowering plants on a country road that wound through the jungle. A station wagon passed them on its way down, with six surfboards sticking out the back.

"Oahu is the sun and surf capital of the Hawaiian Islands," Jeff read from a brochure he had picked up at the airport. "Hike through the rainforests, bike along the mountain ranges, or swim and surf in the azure blue waters of the Pacific."

"It didn't mention the Polynesian chicks?" Doug broke into a smile. "Man, wait until you see the North Shore. It's incredible."

They pulled over at a small overlook and stopped.

"You can't really absorb the North Shore down at sea level," Doug said. "Take a look."

"Wow," Jeff said, stepping out of the van and taking in the view of the bright blue water, with bigger waves than the average ones in Southern California. The cobalt sea splashed pristine whitewater. Surfers sat on their boards, chatting between sets. A couple of good-sized waves humped up and several surfers turned, paddling straight toward the peak. He turned to Doug and said, "That must be a twelve-foot wave!"

"Not over here," Doug replied. "The locals call that a four-or-five-footer. They judge it by the back of the wave."

"This is a dream, man."

"Or a nightmare," Doug answered, laughing. "For me, anyway. I can't surf as good as you."

They climbed back into the van and continued driving.

"Paul is coming in later today," Doug mentioned. "I told him to meet us on the beach at Rocky Point. We don't have a place to stay right now, so we'll be sleeping under the stars until we find something."

"No problem," Jeff said. "Let's catch some waves." They headed for the beach. The anticipation of catching some great waves filled Jeff with exhilaration.

The beach was crowded with tourists and locals. The waves ranged in size for every ability level. They stopped by a shop for the daily report of surf conditions. Rocky Point reported three-to-six-foot swells.

"Perfect," Jeff said. He sat and watched the surf for a few minutes to see what everybody was doing, where they paddled out, and where the waves were breaking. He paddled out, scanned the horizon, and waited his turn.

"Here comes a set!" another surfer shouted. Jeff spun his board around and got into position.

"Go!" a local shouted, thinking Jeff would miss it.

He took two strokes, and felt the thrill of paddling fast for a wave and feeling it lift the board. He slid to his feet, and to help with the fear, silently repeated his mantra while dropping down the vertical wall. As he hit the water at the bottom of the drop, he banked into the bottom turn to gain speed. He drew a long line by climbing and dropping, making zigzags on the wave. Salt spray stung his eyes as he paddled out again and again on the clear blue water.

Later, on the beach, he sat down beside a golden-tanned girl and struck up a conversation. She mumbled something about looking for God.

"Didn't you see the fire? Satan said he would kill me." Her voice shook and her eyes widened with terror.

Jeff realized she was tripping on LSD. He tried talking calmly to her, but she interrupted him.

"Where's God?" she asked in a panic. "Maybe He can protect me." She stared out at the ocean. "Is there really a God?"

Jeff tried to talk her down by telling her about the path to self-knowledge and some of his beliefs.

"Yeah, but do you believe there's really a God?" She turned and tried to focus on Jeff's face.

"I believe that we need to open our minds to multiple realities and new views of the universe," he said. "Acid helps the brain produce religious revelation."

She started freaking out and cried, "I feel like I'm losing my mind."

Jeff tried to calm her down, but she yelled at him, "Is there really a God?" She grabbed his arm and asked him again. "I need to know." The sharp edge of hysteria forced her voice higher. "Is there a God?"

"I don't know. I can't tell you."

"But ... I need ... to know." Her words choked out between sobs.

Suddenly uncomfortable, he jumped up and started walking away, then turned and said, "Hey, I hope you make it."

He left her sitting alone on the clean white sand—stoned out of her mind, curled up in a fetal position, crying.

Chapter

3

Home Sweet Home

Jeff and Doug were joined by their friend Paul late in the afternoon.

"Where are we staying?" Paul asked.

"I have a small pup tent," Doug offered.

"That means we sleep under the stars."

Looking for a spot to set up camp, they came across an old, abandoned van in an area between two houses near the edge of some trees. They stopped to check it out.

"This could be our new home," Jeff said, walking around the van.

Paul looked inside. "It's infested with mosquitoes, and there's vegetation growing in there."

"Yeah, but it's free." Jeff grinned.

They asked around the area if anyone knew whose van it was. No one knew. It had been there a very long time. Then they divided the van in half and started sweeping, cleaning, and scrubbing. Jeff organized his area, arranged his clothes and books, hung up his beads, and lit some incense.

Jeff in the van, meditating in the "lotus" position, 1968.

"Maybe we can shower with the neighbor's hose," said a sweaty and dirty Jeff. "I'll go ask."

21

"Home sweet home," Paul replied as he slapped the mosquitoes biting his arms.

After showering under the hose, they hitched a ride to buy sleeping bags and flashlights at an Army Surplus store. They bought a couple of mosquito punks. When they lit the repellent, smoke quickly filled the van. Opening the doors was no help, so Doug pitched his tent next to the van.

"I can't sleep in those fumes," Paul said. "Let's sleep on the beach tonight."

They dragged their sleeping bags, flashlights, and books down to the beach, arranging them on the sand.

"Wow!" Jeff said. "There's not a ripple out there. It's like a bathtub tonight." He picked up his stuff and said, "Let's sleep closer to the water where it's cooler."

Jeff's best friend, Paul, 1968.

They stayed awake until two o'clock in the morning talking about Eastern philosophy, chanting and practicing yoga. Jeff didn't remember falling asleep. The next thing he knew, he woke up underwater, choking and sputtering. He scrambled to his feet and tried to get his bearings, when a wave caught him from behind and sent him tumbling. He crawled out of the water, looking for Paul.

"Paul! Where are you?" he shouted.

"Over here!"

Jeff turned and saw him standing in the surf, groping in the water trying to find his flashlight and shoes.

"Our sleeping bags!" Jeff yelled, diving back into the ocean. They retrieved their gear and dragged it up the beach. "These bags must weigh three hundred

22

pounds soaking wet." He collapsed on the sand. Then he remembered Doug.

"Doug!" He looked around. "Doug! Where are you?"

"I don't believe it," Paul said. "Look." He pointed about fifty yards away to a high point on the beach. "He's up there sleeping."

Jeff and Paul woke him up, "What are you doing up here?"

Groggy, he rubbed his eyes. "Man, I felt a wave hit the edge of my sleeping bag, so I moved my stuff up here."

"And you didn't bother to wake us up?" Jeff said.

"It didn't even occur to you to tell us?" Paul added.

"I was tired, man. I figured you'd move."

They went back to the mosquito-infested van. Since there was no bathroom, they used the bushes in the field and the woods behind them. But after awhile, the woods were littered with human waste.

"We have to get organized and do something about this," Jeff decided. They cleaned up the field and dug a hole in the ground. "We'll have our own honey hut."

"This is something you're proud of?" Paul shook his head. "I have to remind myself every day that it's free. That's the only way I can handle it."

Every night when they came back from the beach, they had to light mosquito punks for at least an hour before they could go inside the van. The only cooking utensil they had was a small camp stove to cook rice. Rice and bananas, bananas and rice—it was getting old.

*The gang at Velzyland, North Shore: Jeff, Greg,
Mike (sitting), Keith, Doug, and Jim, 1968.*

4

A House Divided

"I heard about a house available for us to stay at Velzyland Point," Doug said one day.

"Wow! A month of camping out is about all I can take," Paul said.

They packed up their gear and hitched a ride. The road narrowed until they came to a clearing where an isolated two-bedroom communal house sat.

"Mad John owns it," Doug said as they approached the house.

Jeff looked at him. "Mad John?"

"Yeah, he lost an arm. I don't know the story; I just know they call him Mad John. They've been trying to get enough people together to pay the rent. With us, there will be twelve."

"Any girls?" Jeff asked, smirking.

"One," Doug said. "Only one."

"The first thing I want to do after we settle in is catch some waves," Jeff said. Then he grinned. "Well, maybe the second thing. I need a hit."

Stepping inside for a look around, he heard the sound of Janis Joplin music trailing through the house. It looked like what it was—a crash pad. Empty glasses and bottles of wine lay scattered about the living room and kitchen area. Dirty rooms with grease-stained walls and stacks of unwashed, moldy dishes went unnoticed. The sweet smell of grass permeated the house.

"*Aloha!*" one of the guys said in greeting. "I'm Buckwheat." He shook hands with Jeff, then handed him a joint.

"Thanks, man," Jeff said.

Several people sat around the room smoking joints. A few were high on speed. Others were tripping on LSD. Water pipes were scattered across the coffee table. Jeff stayed at the house just long enough to be polite, then headed back out to the beach while it was still daylight.

Later, Jeff ate rice and oats with everyone, then tackled the dirty dishes. He couldn't stand the mess. Afterwards, they sat around smoking pot and talking.

"Watch out for rats tonight," Buckwheat said. "Remember, they're nocturnal."

"Rats?" Jeff asked.

"Yeah, man. Did you know that Hawaii was taken over by rats at one time? The big ones." He gestured with his hands to show the size. "So they got a brilliant idea. Bring in mongooses to kill the rats. But there was a problem they didn't consider."

"What's that?"

"Mongooses sleep at night and come out during the day. Rats sleep during the day and come out at night. So they never saw each other!"

Everyone laughed. The conversation got around to Eastern philosophy and each interjected a viewpoint.

"I think Timothy Leary is on the cutting edge of a revolutionary breakthrough," Jeff declared.

"His ideas and his research are pretty radical," Willy argued.

"Yeah, the establishment shut him down on the LSD research and made it illegal." Jeff shook his head. "Stupid, man. They're afraid of religious revelation."

"What about the Native Americans, the Indians? They used peyote and mescaline in their religious ceremonies. Why should it be illegal now?" Doug chimed in.

"I agree," Jeff said. "But hey, who cares? It's easy to get." He grinned. "At least we've never had a problem getting it."

"Doug tells us that you're on this big search," Buckwheat said. "You're into yoga and meditation?"

Jeff began his lecture, "I think yoga is the best discipline for self-knowledge. There are a lot of different techniques. I've been following Paramahansa Yogananda. He says that we are all part of one spirit. 'When you experience the true meaning of religion, which is to know God, you will realize that He is your Self, and that He exists equally and impartially in all beings.'"[1]

"In other words, we're our own gods?" John asked.

"In a way," Jeff answered.

"We're in trouble," John said, laughing.

"That's why yoga is important," Jeff continued. "So we can get focused and centered. There are different positions for specific goals—to strengthen the body, control the life force, energize and internalize the consciousness. 'Kundalini' is a form of energy that lies dormant at the base of the spine, then is channeled upward through the 'chakras' via yoga. It's like a ladder to spiritual liberation."

"You lost me," Fred said, standing up and stretching. "The only liberation I need right now is my pillow."

"So tell me how you meditate," Willy asked. "What do you do?"

"I burn a stick of incense, play some quiet music, sit in the lotus position, cross-legged on the floor, and chant a mantra to concentrate," Jeff said.

"I think this stuff is a bit far out," Willy said as he headed for the bedroom.

Fred came back to the living room and asked, "Is that some kind of a shrine you set up in your corner of the bedroom?" His voice held an undertone of irritation.

"It's just my books, incense, beads, and stuff," Jeff said defensively. Obviously not everyone was interested in his search or in what he had to say. Suddenly very tired, he headed for his corner and spread out his sleeping bag.

In the morning, Jeff wrote a letter to his mom, dad, and younger brother, Dan.

Dear Family,

Well, here I am and I really can't believe it. It's so beautiful. We found a place to stay with a bunch of us sharing the rent. It's at Velzyland Point, a two-bedroom house. So everything turned out groovy and smooth. I love you all and may God guide you as He is me through the Divine Life.

Adios, Jeff -om-

He then wrote a note to Karyn, a girl he had started dating in the past year but had known throughout high school. He invited her to join him in Hawaii.

Paul and Jeff talked one day about how nice it would be to have real beds to sleep in. But with limited resources,

Karyn's 10th grade photo, 1967.

28

the sleeping bags and four-inch thick mattress pads from the Army Surplus store were all they could afford. What money they had, they wanted to stretch as far and long as they could.

One day flowed into another—surfing, getting loaded, and hanging out, discussing Eastern philosophy. For food, they picked fresh fruit and bought vegetables, but when funds got low, they bought fifty-pound bags of rice and stole large stalks of bananas from nearby fields.

"Guess what we'll be eating for a while?" Doug said sarcastically.

"Rice and bananas are good for you," Jeff protested, trying to be positive. "All natural."

They made banana sandwiches, put bananas in oatmeal, and tried to get creative with a variety of rice and banana mixtures. Breakfast, lunch, and dinner.

"What's for dinner?" became a running joke.

"How about a rice and banana sandwich?" Everyone groaned.

Jeff wrote another letter home, this time asking for money.

Dear Family,

I was sure glad to hear from you. Everything is out of sight here. The surf is up and my board really works groovy. Could you please send me at least fifty dollars? I'm really broke.

Love, Jeff -om-

He wrote Karyn again, disappointed that she wasn't coming.

Dear Karyn,

Did you get my last letter? Hope so. Sure would like to hear from you. What's happening on the mainland, anything exciting? I made some beads, and I'll send them to you. Say "Hi" to everybody.

Love, Jeff -om-

He wrote another letter to his family a week later.

Hello Everyone,

How's everything back home? Hey! The big waves are coming through and they are really strong. They look as big as two-story houses. I've been practicing yoga ever since I got here and I'm really becoming calm. I'm on a really righteous diet and doing a lot of reading.

Love, Jeff -om-

P.S. I cashed the money order you sent, but now the rent is almost due. Can you send something?

Jeff, Paul, Doug, and Mike spent some days up on a hill in a jungle area. They dropped LSD and walked around nude, swinging from trees, acting like monkeys. On other days, they sat around the house chanting. Sometimes they managed to hit the same tone of "Om" and got off on that.

"Whoa!" Paul said. "Did you hear that?"

"We did it!" Jeff said. "We hit that note. Wow."

They practiced yoga for hours, twisting and positioning their legs in different configurations, then turning upside down.

"Talk about a rush ..." Doug said.

One day a visitor came from Maui representing the Self-Realization Fellowship, and they had a group meeting at the house. Everyone got high and the leader was attempting to get the group to chant in unison. But when he began his tone of "Om," it was so unusual that Jeff, Paul, and the others burst out laughing. When they couldn't get it together, he scolded them.

"Your egos are getting in the way."

One of the visitors that day was a girl who had just arrived on the island. She brought drugs with her to sell so she could make money to live on. This leader lectured and pressured her about the system being one where everyone shared what they had.

"You share what you have, and we'll share what we have," he said. "This will lead you down the path to a direct personal experience of the Divine Consciousness which underlies and upholds all life." He used his most pious tone.

The girl tossed her twenty bags of weed on the table, and the group smoked it all in two days. She was broke, but they let her stay at the house. It was all they had to offer her, except for rice and bananas.

Jeff wrote home again.

Dear Family,

Thank you for sending me the last of my money. I sure needed it. I'm having a real enlightening time over here. I met someone the other day, and he showed me some of his books and S.R.F. lessons. Dan, I need a big favor. Would you go to Mystic Arts World in Laguna Beach and pick up a few books for me? They're by Timothy Leary. "The Psychedelic Experience" and "Psychedelic Prayers" from the Tao Te Ching. I'd like to have my own copies. Mom, could you send some cookies or something? And send me at least twenty dollars. As quick as possible.

Then he added his latest philosophy.

This life is only a delusion, a play; we are the actors. If we play the part righteously, we will find a blissful peace.

Love, Jeff -om-

He scribbled on the outside of the envelope:

(Love – Peace – om)

A response arrived quickly from his sister-in-law, Mary.

Dear Jeff,

I hope you do not consider this letter a lecture. Your letters talk of enlightenment and peace, but I hope you are not deluding yourself. Anyone will feel peaceful when there is no stress or responsibilities and you are in a beautiful environment. Until you can be calm inwardly and do the right thing under adverse conditions, you cannot hope to find the kingdom of Heaven on earth.

As to yoga, I only have one word. Beware! You cannot use anything external to find internal peace. Yoga is backwards. Your body is just a shell. Your mind, your soul, and your emotions should come first. Give up your excuses and justifications and give yourself up to God. If you are really and truly searching, truth and peace will come to you. Right now, you are escaping. I hope someday you find what you are looking for. By the way, what does "om" mean?

Love, Mary

P.S. Cookies will follow this letter.

Another letter arrived. This one was from Jeff's sister-in-law, Kaye.

Dear Jeff,

We were glad to receive your letters. It seems your search in Hawaii is almost as fruitless as your search on the mainland. How are you going to stay there if you've spent all your money? I guess since you have never been made to take responsibility for any of your actions, you think you can go through your whole life like that. Well, someday the blow will come. I know this lecture won't do any good, but I really care what happens to you. I'm concerned about your misadventures.

Love, Kaye

P.S. Write soon. Enclosed is a stamp if you are still speaking to me.

Things at the house were growing restless. A few more people had moved in, supposedly to help with the expenses. But everyone was always broke and calling home for money. Someone bought a stereo and music blared almost non-stop, but no one was listening. Half the group was on uppers, half on downers. Fist fights erupted at times. John Peck, one of the better pipeline surfers, was staying with them. He got so crazy that they threw him out of the house. Literally!

One day Jeff was in the bedroom, meditating upside down in the lotus position and chanting his mantra, when a couple of the guys burst through the door.

"Hey, what are you doing?" one of them asked, tilting his head to look at Jeff.

"What does it look like?" Jeff said. His voice revealed his irritation. "I'm meditating." A scowl of concentration covered his face.

"Cool."

"He's looking through his *third eye* again," they snickered.

"What is that sound you make, a mantra?"

"Yeah, a mantra," Jeff said. "The primeval sound of the universe." His voice was courteous, but patronizing.

"Ooooh," one of them said. "The primeval sound of the universe."

"Don't you guys have any respect? Just barging in here like this?" He slowly stood to his feet. "So much for peace and tranquility." He faced them. "For your information, the mantra is a powerful weapon that helps you to follow the path to self-knowledge."

They glanced at each other, then burst out laughing.

"You guys need to clean up your act," he said with disgust in his voice.

"Clean up *our* act?"

"Yeah," Jeff said. "Those reds are going to snuff you out some day. You ought to get where I'm at—on a higher plane."

"Man, you're crazy if you think you're any better than the rest of us." They left the room, mumbling and complaining. "Who does he think he is? Some guru with the answers to life?"

Frustrated, Jeff went into the bathroom and closed the door. It stank of urine and sweat. Then he went to the kitchen and looked around. The sour odor and grease-stained walls got to him. Someone had smashed an empty wine bottle on the floor, scattering shards of glass everywhere. With everybody high and doing his own thing, no one bothered to clean it up. The reality of the filthy condition of the house hit him. Even the mattresses in the bedrooms smelled sour.

"This is crazy. This isn't living," he grumbled as he paced through the house. "I'm out of here." He sighed in exasperation. "I need to be alone and get my head together."

"Feel free," one of them said.

"Yeah, like we'll miss your philosophical lectures." Jeff borrowed a small tent from one of the guys, took his backpack and some water, and headed for the jungle. But not before getting his hands on the heaviest doses of LSD he could find. As a drug pusher in California, he had taken some heavy doses. He had managed to stay stoned on virtually any drug he wanted. This time, he was on a search. He decided to fast for a few days to get a clear mind. Then he would drop the biggest hit of LSD-25 he had ever taken. He had an occult formula to follow. He didn't realize his dream would soon turn into a nightmare.

Chapter
5

Ultimate Psychedelic Trip

After reading Leary's book, Jeff was convinced that instant access to the wisdom of the ancients could be attained immediately through new rituals and LSD journeys, instead of decades of yoga, astral travel, and guidance through death planes.[2] Determined to meet with the primeval powers and forces and to find the higher reality, he hiked into the jungle of the North Shore until he found a spot to pitch his tent. He dropped the acid, not knowing that it was heavily laced with strychnine.

For two days, he felt like he was going to die. He wretched, vomited, and battled for his life, periodically losing consciousness. The vomit was like liquid heat burning his throat. He felt caught up in a universe of insanity. Suddenly everything was hideous, bizarre, threatening, ugly, and hellish. Fear gripped him. He staggered around, in and out of the tent, groping at plants and trees. He heard breathing and weird sounds ripping through the jungle. The trees appeared to be alive, quivering, trembling, and throbbing with energy. Hostile, threatening voices spoke from the bark of the trees. He had no sense of day or night. The walls of the tent shivered and groaned.

A torrential rainstorm with howling winds hit the jungle, and the sounds of the raindrops hitting the trees and tent were magnified a thousand times. He sat on the canvas inside the center of the tent, hugging his knees, swaying back and forth. His body shivered from the dampness.

Finally, the storm ceased, and the sun pierced through the clouds. The sounds of the jungle, alive and fresh after the rain, seemed to be coming from inside his being. Feeling euphoric, he left the tent and felt carried away with the beauty of the sounds. The colors of the jungle were like liquid, sparkling diamonds, with vivid colors swirling before his eyes. He felt like he was traveling through a vast kingdom of inner space. He lay down on the jungle floor and closed his eyes. He pictured his spirit leaving his body and floating back. He desperately wanted to experience the *clear light* that Timothy Leary talked about. Exhaustion caught up with his body, and he fell asleep.

Hours later, he woke up and discovered stinging bites all over his body. He looked down and saw that he was completely naked, but he didn't remember taking off his clothes. Hundreds of spiders and ants were crawling on him. He jumped up, shouting and slapping himself all over, trying to brush them off. A tremendous panic consumed him. He felt total desperation, thinking he was lost in the jungle and would never get out.

Completely disoriented, he started running as fast as he could. Bushes and tree branches whipped and scraped at his body. Blood trickled down his side. He ran and ran. A large spider web wrapped itself around his body as he crashed through it. He wondered where the spider was. He began screaming and crying convulsively. Terrified, he forced himself to continue thrashing through the thick foliage, tripping and falling as he went. Abruptly, the jungle stopped, but he didn't. He ran right over the edge of a cliff, tumbling over and over, falling down an embankment. Horror filled him, and he thought he was a dead man.

When his bruised body stopped rolling, he landed on a dirt road that ran along the edge of another cliff. He managed to crawl over to the edge and look down. He was overlooking Sunset Beach, Kammie Land, and Pipeline. He lay down and allowed the sun to bathe his skin. After resting awhile, he began to chant, trying to calm down and rid himself of any remaining fear.

As his mantra filled the air around him, he suddenly felt a heavy presence. He chanted louder and louder. As he did, a sense of strength and power rose up within him. He remembered another time when he had felt this power. A fly had landed on him, and he had focused his meditation on overcoming the will of the fly. He hypnotized it to do whatever he ordered. He told it to flip over, then to fly in a circular pattern in the air, and it had.

"If I have the power to control a fly, why not the waves?" he said aloud.

He continued to chant, focusing all his energies on the ocean. He commanded the waves to increase and get bigger until they devoured everyone in the water. He watched as the swells began to grow enormous. Thundering waves crashed against the shore with great force. The surfers were swept off their boards and disappeared into the turbulent water. He even saw the waves wiping out homes along the shore. He felt like a god. He had access to infinite power; he had tapped into the source, the hidden power behind nature.[3]

"I've got it! I've got the power!" he shouted into the air.

The presence he felt left as quickly as it had appeared. Depression suddenly draped over him like a cloud. He stood and slowly walked down the dirt road, finding his way back to the house.

Paul saw him coming down the driveway. He looked at his naked, dirty, scratched, and bloodied body. "What the ...?" He ran over to Jeff and tried to help him.

"Don't touch me," Jeff said. "I ache all over."

"What happened?" Paul asked. "Where are your clothes?"

"I don't know, and I don't care," he moaned. "I feel like I've been to hell and back."

Paul had been worried about his friend. He hesitated, then said, "I've got some news." His tone indicated it wasn't good.

"Later, man," Jeff pleaded. "I need to clean up first."

In the bathroom mirror, Jeff saw a disturbing sight. His long thick hair and beard were wildly frizzy, dirty, and tangled. It looked as if an electric shock had made it stand on end. Dried vomit smeared his face, and his eyes were red-rimmed with dark circles beneath them. Every bone in his body ached. He climbed into the bathtub, allowing the water to wash away the blood, grass, and dirt stains from his skin. "God isn't here," he thought. He felt like he was losing his mind. Paul was waiting for him when he came out of the bathroom.

"We've got to find another place," he said. "The landlord is kicking us out."

"Why?" Jeff asked.

"Look around," Paul said. "Need you ask? He's complaining about the mess and the drugs. And there are too many people staying here. We've got to move."

"You got any money?" Jeff asked. "Because I sure don't."

"I'm tapped out," Paul answered. "Maybe it's time to go back."

From Chicks to Chickens

When Paul suggested they consider going back to the mainland, Jeff said "No! We'll find a place."

"With what? Our good looks?"

Jeff laughed, then remembered three girls they had met from Anaheim. "Come on," he said. "We're going to the beach." His face broke into a smile. "Those three chicks have a place."

"And why would they let us move in with them?"

"Turn on the charm," Jeff said. "We can do this."

They found the girls on the beach, joked around, and talked awhile, then approached them about moving in and sharing the rent. They agreed.

"You're good," Paul said. "But we do need to come up with some money."

Jeff wrote another letter home.

Dear Family,

Thanks for the film and the envelopes you sent. I've moved into another house with some of the guys and three girls from Anaheim. These girls are really taking care of us. They sew, cook, everything. I'm getting some yoga pants and trunks made. I'm looking for work, but there's not much here on the North Shore. My heart tells me from your last letter that you have lost faith in me. Whether you have or not doesn't matter. What matters is that you don't lose faith in the Divine. What we have done will not be lost to all eternity. Everything ripens at its time and becomes fruit at its hour.

I am completely broke. I need to ask you for a loan, for I have no other choice. Please think it over. As I said, I hope to get a job soon. A hundred dollars will get me through.

Love, Jeff -om-

P.S. A spirit filled with truth must needs direct its actions to the final goal. Truth needs to direct its final action.

Jeff settled in at the house and continued his search for truth, reading many books, attending group discussions, getting high on whatever was available, going to parties and surfing. He often hung out at Kammie's store, as did many of the surfers. The owner listened to everyone's problems while they sipped guava juice. Many of the locals, 'kamainas,' resented the 'haoles,' white boys from the mainland, intruding on their territory. That meant *their beach* and *their girls.* Fights broke out often. There were several incidents where a 'haole' was beaten with baseball bats and ended up in the hospital. When surfing, Jeff was always careful to be friendly and not aggressive, patiently waiting his turn.

"Hey, look at this," Paul said one day when Jeff walked in after surfing. "Jimi Hendrix is coming to Hawaii to do a concert. We should go, man."

Jeff picked up the newspaper.

"They call him the new black Elvis," Jeff said. "Listen to this. 'His hair is a foot long, uncombed and stabs the air in every direction.'" He laughed and kept reading. "When he performed at the Monterey Pop Festival, he hopped, twisted, and rolled over sideways without missing a twang or a moan. He slung the guitar low over his swiveling hips, picked the strings with his teeth, thrust it between his hips, and at the end, doused his guitar with lighter fluid and set a match to it."

"My kind of guy," Paul said, laughing.

They found a group going to the concert and hitched a ride with them. It was a beautiful clear night with a full moon. Everyone took tabs of mescaline and hits of LSD. Someone with a contact at the Otani House in Diamond Head, where Jimi Hendrix was staying, said he might be able to get them into the house after the concert.

With the fury of a hurricane, Jimi Hendrix performed a frenzied assortment of funky electronic soul sounds to the charged-up crowd. When he closed the show with "Purple Haze," the crowd was on its feet. Then he rammed his guitar into some amps, and the audience went wild.

The same night as the Hendrix performance there was another concert going on at the park across the street. Jeff, Paul, and some friends went over there when the Hendrix concert was over. They took more mescaline and listened to the local band. Then they heard a rumor that Jimi was coming. He walked across the street with a crowd following. Then he got up on stage and jammed with the band for about an hour. Hundreds of people lay down on the grass in Thomas Square and watched an eclipse of the moon while Hendrix played.

"What a rush, man," Jeff said. "Can you believe this? An eclipse of the moon and Jimi Hendrix on the same night!"

Later, Jeff and Paul got into the Otani House. Jimi's band members, his roadies, and his groupies sat around, told stories, and got high. Jimi finally came home and crashed in the early morning hours. On their way back to Sunset Beach the next day, Jeff and Paul talked about the concert.

"What an incredible night," Paul said. "I'll never forget it."

"I don't know what was better, the main concert or the jamming afterwards," Jeff said.

"Where does he get all his energy? He's a skinny little guy!"

"I heard one of the band members call him 'The Bat' because he stays up all night."

By the time they got back to the house, they were exhausted. They slept all day and then had to face some bad news. The house was splitting up. Some were heading back to the mainland, the rest were going their separate ways. Jeff and Paul couldn't afford to keep the house themselves. Besides, the landlord had already rented it to someone else.

"What now?" Paul asked. "Here we go again."

"I don't know," Jeff said. "Let's catch some waves." He grabbed his board. "We'll think of something."

They found a place to stay with some friends temporarily. One day someone told them that a chicken farm was looking for help. They both applied for work.

"I don't pay by the hour," the owner said. "I pay by the row."

"The row?" they replied.

"Yes. The chickens are in rows of wire cages up off the ground, and their droppings have to be shoveled out and put in a pile in the field. Then we bag it and sell it. I'll pay you twenty dollars for each row."

"Sounds okay," Jeff said. "I think we can handle that."

Then he showed them the cages. They sat about four feet off the ground, with about three feet of chicken manure beneath them. The rows were about two hundred feet long. They both groaned.

"We need the money," Paul said, picking up a shovel. "But this is disgusting."

"I bet they haven't cleaned this stuff out for three years," Jeff said. Then he got a whiff as he lifted his first shovelful. "Oh man ..."

By the end of the first day, they had blisters on their hands and smelled so bad, they figured their clothes would never come clean. They had only finished one row.

"There must be tons of this stuff out here," Jeff moaned. "We need to renegotiate our deal with this dude." They managed to get a small pay raise.

One day the constant loud clucking of the hens got to Jeff, and he shouted as loud as he could, "Shut up!" Amazingly, for just a moment, the chickens froze, and there was silence.

"Wow," Paul said. "You've got the power."

But almost immediately, they started again—thousands of chickens, sitting in their cages, clucking away. Another time Jeff caught a mouse and put it in their food tray. It ran down the row, and the chickens squawked, jumped, and fluttered, hitting the tin roof of the coop, terrorized. Feathers flew in every direction.

"Payback time," Jeff said with great satisfaction.

The only good thing about the job, other than survival money, was the opportunity to steal eggs—one more item to add to their limited menu of rice and bananas. Now they could have egg and Miracle Whip sandwiches for lunch every day. Hawaii no longer felt like paradise, especially after Jeff got hit with his surfboard. His eyelid split wide-open, blood spurting everywhere. At the emergency ward, the doctor told him to stay out of the water for a while. And, after working all day at the chicken farm, he was usually exhausted, sweaty, thirsty, hot, smelly, and tired to the point of exploding. What was the point of all this?

"I've had it man," Paul said to Jeff one day. "I'm heading back to California. There's nothing for me here." He picked up a banana. "I don't want to see another one of these for a long time!"

"But you have to admit, the surfing is great."

"Get real, man. This isn't working. I've got to get on with my life."

"You mean the 'American dream'?" Cynicism came through in Jeff's voice.

"I don't know," Paul rationalized. "I've got some strong connections. Maybe I'll do a few more drug runs, get myself a nest egg, and go back to school."

"Smuggling is pretty dangerous, man."

"But it pays well," Paul said. "Look at us. Everyone is always writing home for money. We're living off the straight world."

Jeff sighed heavily. "I guess I'll sell my board and go back too." His voice was filled with disappointment.

He sold his surfboard to get money for an airplane ticket home, but it wasn't enough. He had to ask his parents for help again.

As he sat in the plane on the runway, waiting to take off, Jeff felt burned out. He had dropped out of the straight world because he didn't see the value in working hard and striving to have material possessions. He and his friends just wanted to live *naturally*. Yet, they had to live off the straight people's money just for the basic necessities. It didn't make sense anymore. There had to be something else. He did miss his family, Karyn, and other friends. Maybe he should just give up this search for the *clear light* and join the straight world. Go for the American dream. A split-level house with a white picket fence, a wife and kids, a van, a dog, and a good job. He had never really given it a shot. Maybe that would fill the void he felt. He leaned back and closed his eyes. "Yeah, that's it. I'll go back to California and walk right into the American dream." Little did he realize that what lay ahead of him was not a dream; it was another nightmare.

1957-1969

Jeff and Dan, 1958.

*Jeff's Warren High
senior picture, 1967.*

*Grandma, Mom,
Jeff, Dad, and
Dan, 1957.*

Chapter
7

Back to the Beginning

Jeff grew up in Downey, California, a suburb of Los Angeles. His father was a stocky, strong pipe fitter and a chain smoker. His mother, a petite brunette, worked at various sales jobs. His older brothers, Richard and Gary, were already out of the house by the time Jeff started school. He and his brother, Dan, who was two years younger, were like a second family.

By the end of third grade, Jeff already began to show signs of trouble. In fact, he repeated a grade because of his poor reading ability. He was too busy getting into mischief. One day he decided to take hot dogs to school for lunch and cook them over an open fire in the bushes on the playground. He got a few of his friends to join him. But the fire got out of hand and before long, the entire field was aflame. They sat on the sidelines excitedly watching the sights and sounds of the firemen and fire trucks.

"Wow, this is cool!" Jeff said to his friends.

"Yeah, unless they find out it was us who started it."

Another time Jeff broke into the kindergarten room and started a fire. Most of the room was gutted by the time the fire was extinguished. This was the first of many trips to the principal's office for him and his mother—for starting fires, smoking cigarettes, using cuss words, looking at dirty pictures, you name it. By the time he was in sixth grade, being suspended had become a routine occurrence.

One night at the dinner table, Jeff's mom spoke to his dad.

"The school called today," she said.

Jeff stiffened.

"What did he do now?" his father asked, glaring at Jeff.

"He drew a nude picture of a girl," his mom answered. Then looking at Jeff, she asked, "Why did you do that?"

Jeff shrugged his shoulders and poked at his food with his fork. He didn't answer.

Grandma, Mom, Jeff, Dad, and Dan, 1957.

"You shouldn't have done it," she said. "Why are you always getting in trouble? You've already been suspended from school three times this year for swearing, pushing kids around, and mouthing off to the teachers. The teacher says that when she told you to go to your seat, you refused."

His mother sighed. "You're only in sixth grade. If you keep getting suspended, you might not graduate. Why don't you just obey the rules?"

Jeff didn't respond, but gave her a defiant look.

"Answer your mother!" his father shouted, pounding the table with his fist.

Jeff jumped, and in the process, knocked over his glass of milk.

His father stood to his feet and started removing his belt. Jeff cringed. He knew he was in trouble now. His dad started whipping him in anger. Jeff tried to scramble away from him, but he was cornered. His younger brother, Dan, silently stared at his food. He didn't want to be next.

"Now dear, there's no need to overreact," his mother said to his dad, trying to calm him a bit. She got up and began dabbing at the spilt milk with a napkin.

"You shouldn't have done it," his father shouted at Jeff as he continued to whip him with the belt. "What is wrong with you?" The belt snapped again. "You think you're above the rules? That you can just do whatever you want?!" A few more swats, and Jeff could feel the welts. He determined not to cry or show emotion.

"Now, go to your room and think about what you've done." His father's voice was drained of emotion. He went back to the dinner table, dragging his belt with him, and said, "I need a drink."

Jeff's mom got him a beer and some whiskey for a boilermaker. She knew it would calm him down. A second one would put him to sleep.

"You can leave the table," she said to Dan. He scrambled off his chair and went to Jeff's room. Jeff had earphones on. He was listening to the Beach Boys singing "Surfin' USA."

"You okay?" Dan asked, tapping him on the shoulder to get his attention.

"Yeah, it was nothing. I'm fine."

"Did you know that your teacher quit because of you? That's what the kids at school are saying. You were throwing stuff around the classroom and yelling and swearing at her."

"I did make her cry," Jeff smirked. "And she ran out of the room."

"Well, she's not coming back."

"She was only a substitute anyway," Jeff said. "No big deal."

He pulled open one of his dresser drawers and reached for a cigarette. Just then, his mother walked in. Jeff slammed the drawer closed.

"What are you two up to?"

"Nothing." Jeff lied. Dan didn't answer.

She walked over to the drawer and opened it. "What's this mess in here?"

She didn't notice the cigarettes.

"Okay, well, we've had enough problems for one night. Your father is tired. And so am I." She walked toward the door, then turned around and looked at Jeff. "Please try to behave, Jeff. It's important to your future that you graduate from school."

When she left the room, Jeff opened another drawer and pulled out a bottle of wine.

"Where did you get that?" Dan asked.

"From the party Mom and Dad had last weekend. They had so much booze, they'd never miss one bottle." He closed the bedroom door and took a long swig. He loved the warm feeling he got from the top of his head to the bottom of his toes.

"You stole that from Mom and Dad?"

"It's not stealing. It was in the house. Just like groceries."

"Oh," Dan said. Then he grinned. "I want some."

"You're too young."

"I am not!"

"You're just a little skinny bean," Jeff teased.

"I am not!"

"Okay, okay. Just be quiet," Jeff said. He held the bottle while Dan took a gulp. He coughed and sputtered, and Jeff laughed at him. "Told you you're too young." He lit a cigarette.

"Let me have one," Dan said, trying to be cool.

"Are you sure?" Jeff took a drag, then handed it to Dan. He inhaled, choked, and coughed. "Guess you need some practice."

Jeff lay in bed that night tossing and turning from the welts, thinking about what his brother had said about stealing. The first time Jeff stole something was in the third grade. He took a toy from the store, and his mother made him bring it back and apologize to the manager. He decided that was easy—not a heavy price to pay. So he started stealing things regularly. If he wanted something, he took it. And usually, he didn't get caught. He stole half of his friend's coin collection. And he would have been caught stealing liquor from a store had he not outrun the clerk. A smug smile came across his face. Drowsy, he yawned and let the wine do its work. He drifted off to sleep.

"Jeff, it's time to get up." His mother shook him. Jeff groaned. It couldn't be morning already.

"Come on. It's Sunday, and you're going to church."

"Why?" Jeff moaned as he pulled the sheet over his head. The wine left him feeling groggy. His head throbbed, his mouth was dry, and he wanted to sleep.

"You need to go," she insisted. "Maybe you'll learn something that will help your behavior."

Raised Presbyterian, his mom didn't attend church herself, but she felt that the boys should go, so she dropped them off for Sunday school. What she didn't know was that Jeff disrupted the classes there just as he did in school. In fact, he stopped going to class and just hid out in the church building, or he went outside and smoked, waiting for her to come back and pick him up.

He sat up in bed and said, "You know, you're hypocritical. You don't go to church. Why should I have to go?"

"Because you need it," she said exasperated. "And watch your tone with me."

"Well, I'm not going," he said. "I'm not going anymore." He rolled over and faced the wall.

"Jeff!" Her voice rose.

He didn't answer. She gave up and left the room.

Jeff's rebellion continued. One teacher at school was an angry man who seemed to look for opportunities to swat the kids. Jeff provided him with many. After each incident, he was even more determined to do things his own way and not let anyone push him around or tell him what to do. His shoplifting increased and he earned spending money by dealing stolen goods. Cigarette smoking and drinking evolved into rolling joints and smoking marijuana. He was now in middle school.

One afternoon, he was rolling joints and smoking in the bathroom at home when his mother knocked on the door. "Are you okay? You've been in there a long time. What's going on?"

"I'm fine," Jeff said, scrambling to gather everything up and hide it. He opened the window to blow the smoke outside. When he opened the door, she was still standing there.

"Look at me," she demanded.

Jeff looked at her. His pupils were dilated, and he had a silly smirk on his face.

"What are you doing?" she asked suspiciously.

"I had a drink. I'm fine."

"You shouldn't be drinking."

"You do," Jeff said defiantly.

"That's different. You're too young."

Jeff went to his room and hid the joints in his sock drawer. He waited until his mother was gone, then called his friends, Doug and Mike.

"Let's meet at Huntington Pier," Jeff said. "I've got something for you."

When he met up with his friends, they went behind the restaurant on the pier, and Jeff pulled out a joint, grinning.

"A cigarette? That's what you've got?"

"This is not an ordinary cigarette," Jeff said, handing it to Doug. "This is going to make you feel good."

Doug took it and puffed.

"No, man, that's not the way you do it." Jeff snatched the joint out of Doug's mouth. "Watch me." He inhaled deeply and held his breath. Immediately he felt the dizzying effects of the weed. Then he broke into a smile and handed the joint back to Doug.

"Cool," Doug said, after he took a drag and handed it to Mike. "It's like being in a slow-motion movie."

Mike started coughing when he tried to inhale. "My throat's burning, man."

Jeff laughed and took the joint. He took a long, slow drag and held it until he thought his head would explode. "Wow!" he said, letting it out. They passed the joint around until it was gone.

"I'm hungry," Doug said. "Let's go inside."

Pushing and shoving each other, laughing at anything anyone said, they created a scene as they entered the restaurant. People glanced their way, shaking their heads.

"We're just a bunch of juvenile delinquents," Doug announced. The boys burst into gales of laughter.

"Let's move this party to my house," Jeff said.

"Won't your mom be suspicious?" Doug asked, giggling.

"She won't be home for hours," Jeff answered.

As they left the pier and walked across the beach, a preacher walked up to them and held out his hand. "Jesus loves you," he said, then handed them a pamphlet.

The boys glanced at each other, smirking.

"Jesus loves us?" Jeff asked in a mocking tone.

"Yes, He does," the preacher said, smiling.

Jeff in junior high, 1964.

"Get out of here," Doug said to him, then reached down and stuffed sand into the man's pant cuffs. The boys laughed, then bumped sideways into him, knocking him over into the sand. They walked away, slapping each other on the back, laughing.

At Jeff's house, the boys went to the garage, which had been turned into a game room with a pool table. "You rack up, and I'll get the beer," Jeff said.

While they were shooting pool, Jeff's younger brother, Dan, came home.

"Can I play?" he asked.

"Sure, kid," Doug answered. "You can play the loser." They burst out laughing.

Jeff came in with the beer. Dan wanted one.

"You're only a kid. A skinny little kid." Jeff ruffled his brother's hair.

"A kid has to grow up sometime," Doug said. "Let him have a beer."

Jeff stood there, looking at his brother. He didn't really want him following in his footsteps.

"Come on ..." Dan said. "I'm going to do whatever I want anyway. You can't stop me."

"Ooooh," the boys snickered.

Jeff handed him a beer.

By the end of his eighth grade year, Jeff had been suspended from school one too many times. The last incident was for approaching one of the girls in school and yanking down her underwear. Humiliated, she reported him to the principal's office.

"We've had it with you," the principal said to Jeff. His voice was barely able to contain his anger. "You're disruptive and totally disrespectful. You're out of here."

"You mean I'm suspended?" Jeff asked, thinking he might get a week off out of this one.

"No. I mean, you're out of this school system. You're expelled. Get out." He pointed to the door for Jeff to leave. "I'll be talking to your mother."

Jeff left the school and didn't go home until later that night. It was dinnertime, and his father was waiting for him. He had already had a drink or two.

"How many times? How many times do we have to go through this with you?" Jeff's father stood to his feet, knocking over his chair as he did. He towered over Jeff, and his muscles strained against the fabric of his shirt. "When is this all going to end?" The anger in his voice rose an octave. "Do you realize what you're doing to your mother and me?"

Jeff didn't respond. He hung his head, looking down at his feet.

"Look at me!" his father shouted. "Do you even care? No! All you care about is yourself and what you want. You're not thinking about how your actions are affecting others." His anger intensified.

"Now dear," Jeff's mother said. "Let's talk about this." Then she looked at Jeff. "Your father and I have a plan."

"But first," his father interrupted, "I need to teach you some respect." He began removing his belt.

Jeff decided not to stick around for the beating. He dashed through the dining room and headed for the door. His father turned to go after him and crashed into the table, causing dishes and food to fly in every direction. Jeff's mother screamed. Jeff was out the door in a flash, his father chasing after him. But Jeff was quicker, and his father had to slow his pace, finally coming to a stop. His chest pounded. He could hardly breath. Completely exhausted, he slowly walked back to the house.

"Are you okay?" his wife asked.

"I'm fine," he answered. He went into the house and made himself a drink.

Jeff stayed out until he was sure everyone had gone to bed. Then he slipped back into the house and went to his room. He lay on his bed staring at the ceiling. Maybe he should just run away, take off.

He remembered when he was six years old and did just that. He ran away with a twelve-year-old boy in the neighborhood. They hiked along the riverbed, and Jeff's feet were bleeding because his little cowboy boots were too tight. And they were hungry. So they made their way to a main road, where a man picked them up and offered them a ride. He invited them to stay at his house. Frightened, Jeff started to cry and told the man that he didn't want to go. He wanted to go home.

He raised a big fuss, so the man dropped him off at a bus station. He gave him just enough change for a ticket back to Downey, then left him there, alone. Jeff stood by himself crying until a woman came over and asked what was going on. She called the police, and Jeff was brought home in the police cruiser. His parents were so glad to see him. He got lots of attention. He remembered how good that hot bath felt and how well he slept that night. Later he found out that this guy's intention was to sexually abuse both of them. His friend managed to escape from the man's house before anything happened. Maybe running away wasn't such a good idea.

There was a tap on his bedroom door. "Jeff? Are you in there?" It was his mother.

"Yeah, I'm here."

She came in and sat on the edge of his bed. "Jeff, we've talked with your brother, Gary. He's willing to have you come live with him for a while."

"In Santa Ana Canyon?"

"Yes. You'll be living with Gary and Kaye and going to school there. I think you need to get away from some of the friends you hang out with and start over in a new environment."

"What if I don't want to go?"

"You don't have a choice this time," his mother said in a firm voice. "You're going." She sighed. "Your father and I have discussed it and that's it. We don't know what to do anymore." She choked back the tears. "You're going." She got up and left the room.

Jeff lay in the dark listening to his mother softly weeping in the other room. "Maybe she's right," he thought. "Maybe if I hang out with a new group of friends in a new school, things will be better." If his brother cared enough to take him in, then the least he could do is try.

The Young Rebel

Jeff entered ninth grade at the new school and made a point of finding out who the smart kids were. His plan was to hang out with them and stay out of trouble. He joined the track team, then the basketball team. The basketball team actually won the championship for their district. But slowly, Jeff gravitated back toward the kids that drank and partied—the surfers. He got his first surfboard at age ten and had been surfing ever since.

He and his brother, Dan, won many surf contests over the years, gaining reputations among the inland surf group. They were good. When Jeff was out on the water, he felt free. But surfing wasn't enough. Alcohol and drugs had a strong pull on him. Before long, he was stealing again to get extra spending money. He dressed different, his hair got longer—and he started to have run-ins with his brother.

"What are you doing?" Gary asked him one day, grabbing Jeff's hands and looking at his long fingernails. "Your nails look like a girl's," he said in disgust.

"What's wrong with growing my fingernails?" Jeff asked. "Just because you're a Navy man doesn't mean I have to be," he said in a flippant tone.

Jeff and Dan, 1958.

"You're going to cut them short like a man," he ordered.

"No, I'm not."

"Yes, you are," Gary said, his anger rising.

"You can't make me cut them," Jeff said in defiance.

Gary lost it. He lunged for Jeff and slammed him up against the wall.

"You're going to do what you're told," he said through clenched teeth.

Jeff felt a surge of rage. Nobody was going to push him around. Nobody.

"Get your hands off me!" He pushed his brother away from him with such force that Gary sprawled out on the floor. He quickly scrambled to his feet and pounced on Jeff full force, fists swinging. They both tumbled around the room, knocking things over.

"I've had it with you!" Gary shouted. "You're already in trouble at school and you just won't listen to anyone. You have no respect. What kind of an example do you think you're setting for my kids?" He walked toward the door, then turned back. He pointed his finger at Jeff and said, "I give up on you. At the end of the school year, you're out of here. Do whatever you want." He slammed the door behind him.

Sent back home to his parents at the end of ninth grade, Jeff called his old buddies, and they picked up right where they had left off. They spent the summer smoking dope, drinking, stealing, and chasing girls. One day a friend said he had a surprise for Jeff.

"We've got something planned. Get yourself over here." He laughed and hung up before Jeff could say anything.

When Jeff arrived at his house, several other friends were there.

"Come on," they said. "We're going for a ride."

"Where?" Jeff asked. "What's going on?"

They all laughed and said, "It's a surprise."

They pulled up in front of a house and said, "Go knock on the door, Jeff."

"Come on, guys, what's all this about?" Jeff asked.

"Just knock." They tumbled out of the car and pushed Jeff towards the door.

Jeff tapped on the door and an older, sensually dressed girl greeted him.

"Come on in," she said in a seductive voice. Jeff's friends snickered in the background.

"It's party time!" they shouted, stumbling through the door.

The girl took Jeff by the hand and led him into the bedroom. When Jeff came out, one of his friends went in. One at a time, they all took a turn.

Later, Jeff asked the others, "Who is she? How did you find her?"

"We paid her."

"She's a prostitute?" Jeff asked, trying not to act too shocked.

"Well, don't look so surprised, man." Then his friend grinned. "It's your inauguration into a long, hot summer."

"Yeah, man, but from now on, we don't pay," another said. "There are plenty of chicks out there who want it."

Jeff spent that summer surfing, dating a variety of girls, increasing his drug use, and getting into more trouble.

Most of his friends were from Downey High School, even though he attended Warren High on the south side of town.

Many of them had older brothers who were into heavy drugs. They soon made their way to Jeff and his friends. Jeff tried the jock thing in tenth grade and even made the varsity wrestling team, but within a few months, he was bored.

He dropped off the team and started hanging out in Hollywood around the head shops—boutique stores that sold hippie-style clothes, beads, candles, incense, jewelry, and drug paraphernalia. He met some guys there who were smuggling drugs in from Mexico. He bought drugs from them, then sold them at school. At one point, they made him an offer to get involved with the smuggling to increase his income, but Jeff decided against it. That was a bit too dangerous for him. He only cared about having enough money to stay high and party.

One day he went with a group of friends to Disneyland. They took some alcohol and drugs inside, and before long, they were causing a scene. At one point Jeff went up on stage where the entertainers were performing. He grabbed the microphone and started singing "California Girls." Within minutes, security guards surrounded him, dragged him off the stage, and marched him to the underground offices.

"Wow, I never even knew this existed," Jeff said. "There's a whole city down here."

A security officer called his house, and his mother came to pick him up.

"You can't even behave at Disneyland?" his mother accused. "When is all this going to end?"

Jeff didn't answer, and they drove home in silence.

On the weekends, a favorite hangout was along the Colorado River. Hundreds of teenagers went there to swim, water ski, float down the river, and get high. At night, they started campfires. Sometimes the Hells Angels came through on their motorcycles. They always had a supply of drugs.

"Hey, kid," one of them called over to Jeff. "Try some of these." He laughed as he tossed a bag of reds on a picnic table.

Everybody crowded around, grabbing what they could. They were already high, and within a short time, people were shouting, laughing, and getting rowdy.

Then the sound of shattering glass pierced the air. Someone took a rock and smashed a car window.

"Hey! That's my car!" somebody shouted from across the parking area. Anger surged, and he ran towards the kid who had smashed the window. Suddenly, all hell broke loose. There was punching, kicking, and cursing. Fights broke out in small groups, with fists flying and blood spurting. Some kids began smashing car headlights with baseball bats. Others threw broken bottles and rocks. Jeff was right in the middle of it all. Within minutes, many of the cars had gaping holes in the windshields and dents everywhere. Jagged pieces of broken glass littered the area and gleamed in the moonlight. It had turned into a full-blown riot.

Finally, someone called the cops. The piercing sound of sirens broke it up, and soon police were swarming everywhere. Jeff thought it was all a big joke, until he felt the cold steel and click of handcuffs around his wrists. The police arrested him and tossed him into a cruiser. They were on the Arizona side of the river, and the jail was worse than Jeff thought it would be. Overcrowded with Native American drunks, drug addicts, and robbers, the place was a nightmare. Racism between whites, Mexicans, and Native Americans increased the tension.

One inmate, a muscular man with a long, thick ponytail, had a dark, troubled look. He strutted around the cell looking for someone to fight. Jeff stayed in a corner, away from the other inmates. He tried to act cool, but a knot of fear gripped his stomach. Cockroaches scurried everywhere, and the odor of sweat and urine permeated the concrete and steel cell. When Jeff was finally allowed to make a phone call, he got through to his mother and asked her to bail him out. She refused to drive to Arizona, but she arranged to send five hundred dollars via Western Union. It took three days to get everything taken care of. Jeff didn't sleep much with bugs and cockroaches crawling over him each night.

A short time later, Bobby, an acquaintance from high school, was at one of the river gatherings. He got high and drove his car off the river embankment. His death was reported on the news the next day. Another friend slipped off a barge; everyone was so loaded that they didn't fully realize what was happening. Jeff remembered seeing Roy sitting there, and the next thing he knew, he had slipped off and disappeared into the river. At the funeral, Jeff fought back the tears at first, but then felt it was all surreal—just like when Kennedy got shot. Everyone was always talking about Kennedy's assassination and getting upset about it. Jeff cracked jokes instead.

"What's the big deal?" he said flippantly.

"You're so cold," one of the girls replied. "How can you not be upset over our President getting shot?"

"It's not like he was my personal friend," Jeff said, walking away from the conversation. Even some of his friends got angry with him over that one.

The deaths at the river didn't slow Jeff and his friends down for long. They continued to party and use drugs—amphetamines, reds, rainbows, and LSD. One night, a buddy picked him up in his black 1946 Ford.

"Are you ever going to fix this thing?" Jeff asked as he climbed in.

"It gets me where I need to go. That's all I care about," he said.

"Look at the headliner. It's all torn and hanging down."

"Hey, at least I've got wheels." He glanced over at Jeff. "More than you can say right now."

They picked up some girls and some drugs, then went joyriding to Dana Point and to a portion of road on Pacific Coast Highway called "Blood Alley." A pounding rain fell from the gray sky, making the pavement slick. Bob pressed down on the accelerator, and the speedometer kept climbing. The car swerved and slid from side to side.

"Go, Bob, go!" one of the girls shouted. She was feeling no pain.

Everyone laughed, and Bob turned up the volume on the radio. "The End" by The Doors blasted from the speakers. They had several near-accidents before the night was over. From time to time, Jeff was overcome by the terrifying fear that they were going to crash and die. Once the drugs kicked in, it just didn't matter.

Jeff floated back and forth between friends like Paul and others from Downey and his buddies at Warren. With the rivalry between schools, and the additional rivalry between surfers and greasers—the beer drinkers who worked on their cars and motorcycles—Jeff often ended up in the middle of fights. One group hung out at McDonalds and another at Mr. G's, each protecting their territory. There were lots of drug transactions and people hanging out, getting high. Confrontations and challenges often led to violence. Anytime someone was looking for a fight, all he had to do was drive into the other group's territory. Male or female, it didn't matter. You just didn't cross the line unless you wanted trouble.

One day four girls from Warren High drove through Mr. G's parking lot, taunting the boys hanging out there. Jeff and his friends jumped in front of the car and surrounded them. The girls panicked.

"Go!" one of them shouted at the girl driving. She slammed her foot on the accelerator, but instead of lurching forward, the car stalled, then died.

"You trying to run us over?!" Paul shouted. "Are you crazy?" He and the others started bashing the car. Some stomped on the hood, others smashed the headlights and doors with baseball bats. One grabbed an ax and slammed it through the roof, penetrating the metal. Terrified, the girls screamed.

"Help! Please! Somebody help!"

By the time police arrived on the scene, the car was demolished.

Another time Jeff, Doug, and Mike drove to where the greasers were working on their cars.

"Hey, you good-for-nothing greasers," Jeff yelled out the window as Mike slowed the car to a crawl. "Haven't you got anything else to do?"

"They don't have brains for anything else," Doug chimed in.

The greasers glanced at each other, then slowly moved out to the street, surrounding the car. "Well, if it ain't the pretty boys," one of them mocked. "On your way to the beach to work on your tan?" The others hooted and howled.

"Yeah, you wish you knew how to surf," Jeff said. "You're just a bunch of wannabes."

"We don't let anyone talk to us like that," one of them warned.

"Is that right?" Jeff said. "And what are you going to do about it?"

Before they realized what was happening, Jeff and Doug were yanked out of the car and slammed down on the ground. They were outnumbered four-to-one.

"What's the matter, surfer boys? Can't get up?"

Jeff struggled to his feet and someone whacked him across the back with a lead pipe. He felt a sharp pain and collapsed face down on the pavement. The boys roared with laughter and started kicking, cursing, and screaming. When it was over, Jeff and Doug half crawled, half walked back to the car, tripping over each other.

"That's a warning," one of the greasers said. The sound of his voice showed that he meant business. "Don't come around here with your big mouth." He pointed his finger at Jeff's bloody face. "Or it will be worse next time." His breath reeked of beer.

As they drove away, Jeff heard someone say, "Well, the pretty boys ain't so pretty anymore." They gave each other a high-five and howled with laughter.

"I think my nose might be broken," Jeff groaned.

"Man, that was the worst," Doug said. "I hurt all over."

They drove in silence for a while, then Doug changed the subject and said, "You've been seeing a lot of Debbie lately. You're not getting serious are you?"

"Serious? Me?"

"Come on. You two are definitely an item."

"Yeah," Jeff grinned. "I guess you could say that." They pulled into the driveway at Jeff's house.

"Oh no," Jeff said. "My brother Dick is here. Time for another lecture." He got out of the car and limped toward the house.

Chapter
9

Party Animal

"What in the world happened to you?" Dick asked when Jeff walked in.

"Nothing," Jeff said.

"What kind of an answer is that? Look at you. You're a mess. What happened?"

"Don't ask." Jeff walked over to the kitchen sink to wash his hands, then got some ice from the freezer, wrapped it in a towel, and held it against his nose. "What are you doing here?"

"I want to talk to you."

Jeff groaned.

"Listen, you could have so much going for you," he said. "You're a good-looking, bright kid. But you're heading in the wrong direction."

Jeff groaned again. "Just leave me alone."

"Don't you want to do something with your life?"

"I am doing something. Leave me alone."

"There's someone I want you to listen to," Dick said. His excitement was reflected in his voice. "Roy Masters. He has a radio show and he does seminars on self-realization and how your mind can keep you well. He uses hypnosis to calm people down and get them to meditate."

"You want me to try that?" Jeff asked in surprise.

"I just want you to hear this guy. He's good, and I like what I've heard him say." He looked into Jeff's eyes and knew he was high. "You could use a little peace in your life."

"I'll think about it," Jeff said, too tired to argue.

Jeff's other brother, Gary, also tried to help him. One day he came over and said, "I have a proposition for you. How would you like to have a car?"

Jeff perked up. "What are you talking about?" He was hurting for transportation.

"I'll make a deal with you. When you stayed with us, I got to see some of your drawings. You're a good artist. I think you ought to develop that talent."

Jeff sighed.

"There's an ocean scene I'd like to have you paint for me, and I'll have it framed. If you can get it done in the next thirty days, I'll give you four hundred dollars to buy a used car. It will teach you to set a goal and complete it on time."

Jeff wanted his own car, so he accepted the challenge. He started the painting, but didn't finish it within the allotted time. He was too preoccupied with parties and drugs. Eventually, he did complete it for his brother. But the deal was off with the car. He later managed to get enough money to buy an old Fiat for fifty dollars. It wouldn't go over thirty miles per hour. His mother was happy about that!

Jeff took Debbie to a dance at school where the Beach Boys were performing hits like "Surfin' USA" and "I Get Around." Afterwards, they spent most of the night parking and making out. They had been dating exclusively for a while. At least that's what Jeff thought. Then he heard rumors that she had been seen with someone else. One night when they were parked outside her house, Jeff confronted her.

"I heard you were seeing someone else," he said.

"What?" She looked down. "No way."

"Why would my friends lie to me about something like that?"

"I don't know." Then she looked at him. "Why do you believe your friends and not me?" She acted insulted and got out of the car, slamming the door.

"Debbie, let's talk about this," Jeff pleaded. He got out of the car. But she had already opened her front door and slipped inside the house.

Jeff tossed and turned that night. He just knew she was cheating on him. The next day he asked her out, but she said she had something to do. Suspicious, Jeff hid in the bushes across the street from her house, waiting for her to come home. High on reds, he was looking for a confrontation.

A car came down the street and pulled over. Jeff could see Debbie inside with another guy. Anger blazed in his eyes as he watched for a few minutes, then charged across the street up to the car. The windows were rolled down and he managed to reach into the driver's side and grab her date around the neck before he could react. Jeff started choking him.

"Are you crazy?" Debbie screamed.

Jeff opened the door and dragged him out on to the pavement. "Who do you think you are, dating my girl?" he growled at him.

"Hey man, I'm not looking for trouble." He could see that Jeff was out of control.

"Well, I'm going to teach you a lesson," Jeff said, punching him full-force in the gut. The kid let out a "whooofff" of air and grabbed his stomach.

Debbie scrambled out of the car, screaming. "Jeff! Stop it!"

Jeff struck him again.

Debbie jumped on Jeff and started pounding him with her fists. "Leave him alone!"

All the screaming and fighting caught the attention of some neighbors.

"What's going on out there?" someone yelled.

"Call the cops," another neighbor shouted.

Soon the wail of police sirens could be heard coming towards them. Jeff let the guy go and took off running down the street, dodging between houses. When he finally stopped to catch his breath, he thought, "How could she do that to me? She lied to me. She's probably been seeing him the whole time she's been with me." His stomach was clenched tight. He waited until he was sure the police were gone, then he headed to McDonalds.

A whole crowd of kids milled about the parking area. Jeff's clothes were torn and dirty from fighting. He walked past someone from a rival school and said to him, "What are you looking at?"

"What's your problem?" the kid said.

"You're the one with the problem." Jeff shoved him backwards.

Other kids crowded around, yelling, "Fight! Fight!" Soon fists were flying everywhere. It turned into a brawl between Downey High and Warren High. Jeff was kicking everyone in sight, cursing, screaming, and striking out with his hands and feet.

Before long, the sound of sirens wailing in the distance could be heard again. Kids jumped into their cars, engines started and tires squealed, as everyone tried to get out of there before the cops pulled in. Jeff kept pounding on one of the kids, his anger raging out of control. Two cruisers sped down the street and pulled into the parking lot. The doors swung open and several police officers swooped down on them. Suddenly, Jeff felt a cop grab him from behind. He slammed him up against the car. Handcuffed, Jeff was tossed into the backseat of the cruiser. The cops left him there while they went to arrest several other teenagers.

Jeff decided to take his chances. He scrambled out of the cruiser and started running as fast as he could. But a cop was right behind him. As Jeff bolted around the corner of the building, he hit a slippery area, lost his balance, and went flying. His head hit the pavement. He tried to scramble back to his feet, but with the handcuffs on, he couldn't do it before the cop came around the corner and pinned him down.

"You're going to jail," he said.

Jeff's parents were called to come down to the police station. They bailed him out, but his father was so angry, he wouldn't speak to him. His mother cried when they got home. Jeff took a shower and went to bed. He lay there staring at the ceiling, still furious at Debbie for cheating on him. The next morning, the local newspaper published a story on the riot.

The following week when things calmed down a bit, Jeff talked with Debbie. She acted as if she wanted to get back together with him. Then she dropped the bomb.

"I'm pregnant," she said. Tears blinded her eyes.

"Pregnant?" Jeff closed his eyes. "Wow ..."

"What should I do?" She choked out the words.

"I don't know." He waited until she stopped crying. "What do you want to do?"

"I can't take care of a baby." Hot tears rolled down her cheeks. "I want to finish school."

"We'll work it out," Jeff said. He took her into his arms. "I'll do the right thing."

"What do you mean?"

"Well, maybe," he hesitated, "maybe we should get married."

Debbie didn't answer.

"Let's just think about it," Jeff said. "I don't know what to do either."

Tormented by confusing emotions, he went home that night and decided to talk to his mother. Even though she didn't approve of his lifestyle, she was a pretty good listener.

"Mom, I've got something to tell you," Jeff said. With a long, exhausted sigh, he sat down on a kitchen chair.

"Now what?" she asked. "Maybe I'd better sit down too."

"It's Debbie. I got her pregnant."

His mother put her head in her hands and fought back the tears.

"I've got to do the right thing. I've got to marry her."

"No, you don't," she said. "Jeff, you're much too young to get married. You have to finish high school. Decide what you're going to do with your life. You can't just get married."

"But she's pregnant. I need to do the right thing," Jeff insisted.

"You amaze me," she said. "You've been so irresponsible, constantly getting in trouble, and now you feel you need to do the right thing and get married?" She shook her head from side to side. "You made one mistake. Don't make another," she said. "You don't love her enough to get married. This is infatuation, not a good foundation for marriage."

The next day Jeff and Debbie talked again. He told her what his mother had said.

"It's okay," Debbie said. "I've made a decision."

"What are you going to do?"

"When I start showing, I'll go up to Saint Anne's Maternity Home for Girls and stay there until the baby is born. I'll just tell everybody I'm visiting a relative or something."

"How will you explain the baby afterwards?"

"There won't be a baby for me to explain."

"What?!"

"I'm giving it up for adoption." She looked at Jeff. "I'm not ready to be a mother and you're not ready to be a father."

Debbie left school about two months later. Jeff went to see her a few times at the maternity home. Then he found out she was still seeing someone else. They argued. He began to realize that the baby she was pregnant with might not even be his. Infuriated and convinced the baby wasn't his, Jeff stopped visiting her.

Karyn in high school, 1968.

Not quite able to get over it, he stopped by Karyn's house one day. She was Debbie's close friend and she was easy to talk to. They had double-dated a number of times.

"Can you believe she's giving up her baby?" Jeff said to Karyn. "Can you imagine anybody doing such a thing?"

Karyn was quiet, then said, "Why did you call it *her* baby? What about you?"

"I don't believe it's mine anymore."

"I think you're wrong," Karyn said. "It's yours."

"How could she be seeing two of us at the same time?"

"Like you never did that?"

"I didn't do that with her. And I didn't lie about it."

"Of course, and that makes it okay." She shook her head. "You guys have a double standard. We're supposed to be faithful to you, but not the other way around."

"Well, I guess it doesn't really matter anymore because Debbie is seeing someone else." He sighed. "It's over between us." He looked over at Karyn. "You're pretty easy to talk to, you know."

"That's me. Everybody's friend." She smiled at him.

"I heard you and Mike broke up."

"Yeah, it's just as well. He was a control freak."

"What do you mean?"

"I don't really want to talk about it," she said, feeling uncomfortable.

"What about my brother, Dan? You dated him a few times."

"We just went a few places as friends. Nothing more."

Changing the subject, he asked, "Have you ever thought about God?"

"Sure. I was raised Baptist."

"That doesn't mean anything. My parents are Presbyterian, but they never go to church, and they don't seem to know how to find God."

"What brought all this on?"

"My brother, Dick, told me to listen to Roy Masters' radio program. Your mind can keep you well. Self-realization. It's like there's a god within us if we can just tap into it."

"So now you're on a God-search?"

"There must be something out there. I'm just curious. I've been listening to this guy and a lot of what he says makes sense. You should listen to him sometime."

Chapter

10

Searching for Something More

Jeff began spending more time with Karyn. He was always comfortable around her and he felt welcome at her house. Her mother especially liked Jeff because he was always smiling and friendly when he came in. She had no idea that he was into drugs and drinking. Most of his surfer friends from Warren were drinkers, but didn't get heavy into drugs. His friends from Downey were the druggies. Jeff was heavy into both. He went to shooting galleries where some of his friends shot up, but when it came to needles, Jeff held the line. It kept him away from heroin.

Hanging out in Hollywood, he became fascinated with Eastern philosophy and the hippies who were into meditation and the yoga movement. They talked about Nirvana and the awakening of the soul's "eternal consciousness." Jeff shared his discussions and thoughts with his mother.

"What do they believe?" she asked.

"That we've lost touch with our original, pure consciousness and have forgotten our true identity," Jeff said. "By following '*dharma,*' we can be free from anxiety and enter into a state of enlightenment." He relished using the new terminology. "Krishna is the eternal father of all living beings, and he is sustaining the entire cosmic creation."

"Don't they believe in reincarnation?"

"Yes. Life does not begin at birth or end with death. The soul migrates from one body to another." Her interest kept him talking. "And they meditate and chant to relieve the mind of anxieties."

"Well, I sure can't picture you chanting," his mother said. "And some of them shave their heads." She grinned at Jeff. "You've got a pretty thick head of hair."

"Don't worry," he said. "I'm not shaving my head or wearing a robe. I don't know what I believe," he continued, "but some of what they say makes sense. It fits in with some of the things Roy Masters says in his lectures about how your mind can keep you well. He also talks about the truth and the light."

"I'm glad you're thinking about these things," she said. "But I wish you would pay as much attention to your school books." She sighed. "I'm worried about your grades."

"Don't worry, I'll graduate," Jeff said. "It's just all so boring." He went up to his room and decided to try the chant. He sat on the floor, legs crossed in the lotus position, back straight, hands resting on his knees. He closed his eyes in order to concentrate.

"Om ... om ... om ..." he chanted, as he meditated on his third eye.

Try as he did, he couldn't focus. His mind kept wandering to the gathering coming up in Malibu Canyon. It was going to be a big bash. Bands, girls, peace, and love. In fact, they called it a "love-in," meaning nudity, sex, drugs, and alcohol. Wherever the music was rockin' and the action was happening, that's where he wanted to be. Eastern philosophy could wait.

By the time Jeff got there with his buddies, the canyon was booming with music by Country Joe and The Fish, Bob Dylan, and others. When bands weren't playing, car radios blasted out the Jimi Hendrix classic "Purple Haze," The Doors singing "Light My Fire," and Jefferson Airplane's

"Somebody to Love." Nude girls and guys walked around, handing out flowers, saying "peace and love." Drugs were everywhere—marijuana, LSD, uppers, downers, whatever anyone wanted. Beer and hard booze were emptied out of the ice chests. The event lasted well into the night, until too much liquor and drugs started to do their work. Fights broke out; beer bottles flew through the air, smashing on rocks, cars, and people. Soon the police sirens echoed through the canyon and everyone was told to leave. That night they didn't bother to arrest anyone.

While Jeff partied at Malibu Canyon, his brother Dan had gone to Disneyland with some friends. At times Jeff tried to discourage Dan's drug use, but he ended up following Jeff's example. When Jeff got into heavier things like LSD, Dan did the same. On this particular night, they had gotten a bad batch with strychnine in it, and Dan couldn't come down. Terrified, he checked himself into the emergency ward of the hospital. His parents spent the night at his side. Later in the morning, they called Jeff to tell him about Dan.

"Wow, I hope he makes it," Jeff said. The ringing phone had woken him from a sound sleep.

"That's it?!" His mother lowered her voice to a whisper. "You hope he makes it?"

"Well, yeah. I do hope he makes it," Jeff said. "Is there anything I can do?"

"He's following in your footsteps," his mother said, her voice breaking up.

"He made his own choices," Jeff said a bit defensively. "Do you want me to come to the hospital?"

"Never mind," she said, holding back tears of disappointment. "There's nothing you can do now. We just have to wait and see how he comes through this."

85

Jeff went back to bed and stared at the ceiling. He thought about the times he had tried to keep things from his brother. He really didn't want Dan imitating him. But Dan was persistent and Jeff gave in. He introduced him to the whole drug scene. Now he lay in a hospital bed, possibly hovering between life and death. Jeff got up and took some pills to dull his thoughts. After his stay at the hospital, Dan was sent to his brother Dick's for a while and placed in therapy. It would be a long time before he was well again.

Jeff drove to Karyn's house. He needed to talk to someone.

"I feel bad about Dan," Jeff said, "even though I know he made his own choices." He looked over at Karyn. "Do you know how many times I ripped him off? I remember one time I borrowed his surfboard, then wrecked it." He hung his head. "And I'm always taking his clothes." His voice trailed off. His thoughts fluctuated from feeling responsible for Dan because of the lousy example he had set to realizing that his kid brother had made his own decisions.

"Sounds like a big guilt trip to me," Karyn said. "Or a pity party." She touched Jeff's shoulder. "You're right. He made his own choices. There's nothing you can do."

Jeff's eyes studied Karyn's face. "You sure know how to make someone feel better." He resisted the temptation to hug her.

Karyn picked up on the gleam of interest in his eyes. Her cheeks became warm and she was angry with herself for being embarrassed. He was on the rebound from dating her friend, Debbie, and she was on the rebound from Mike. She didn't really want to get involved with anyone, although she was attracted to him.

"Graduation is coming soon," she said, changing the subject. "What are your plans afterwards?"

"Actually, I'm glad you brought that up," Jeff said. "Because there may be no afterwards if there's no graduation."

"What's going on?"

"My grades. They're not going to cut it. I'm failing."

"Wow," she said.

"I was wondering ..." Jeff reached out for her hand. "You work in the office at school. Is there any way you can access my grades?"

"What are you asking me?" she inquired suspiciously.

"You could see to it that I graduate," he said. "I'd be grateful."

"How grateful?" She said it without thinking, then awkwardly laughed it off. "Let me check it out."

Karyn managed to get into Jeff's files at school, changed his failing grades to just-passing ones, and forged teachers' signatures. No one noticed, so Jeff graduated along with 758 other students from Warren High School.

Jeff didn't know what he wanted to do after graduation, but about one thing he was sure—he didn't want to go to Vietnam. The country was in the middle of college riots, antiwar demonstrations, and the burning of draft cards and the American flag. One day he was sitting around with his friends, Mike, Charlie, Paul, and Doug. They were all concerned about the draft.

"They've got a half-million American forces over there," Charlie said. "Why do they need us?"

"I heard an interview with a private in the Army," Mike said. "He claimed that Vietnamese cigarettes are cheap and easy to get over there."

"What are they?"

"Cartons of pre-packaged, pre-rolled marijuana cigarettes soaked in opium."

"I heard you can get liquid opium, speed, acid, anything you want over there," Paul said. "But we can get that here too. So what's the big deal?"

"Listen," Jeff said, "I don't want to go to Vietnam because I don't want to get killed. Period."

"So what are we going to do about the draft? Now that we're out of school, we're Class I-A, and we have to report to the local Selective Service Board."

"I've got an idea," Jeff said. "Work with me on this."

They went down to the induction office later that week, each high on mescaline. They were expected to have physicals to qualify for the military. They each had a plan. Paul told them he had high blood pressure and started acting crazy. The doctor doing the interview tried to stay calm and continued to ask questions. Paul jumped up and shouted, "Okay! Okay! I admit it. I use heroin." Then he grabbed the table in front of the doctor, picked it up, and threw it across the room. Papers and files flew in every direction. "You got a problem with that?" Horrified, the doctor had him tossed out of the office.

Two of them walked into the office, lingered around as if they were waiting their turn, and casually poked through files, looking for theirs. It was so busy that no one noticed. They found their folders, casually picked them up, and went to the restroom. There, they stuffed them inside their shirts, came out, and strolled out of the office. They never heard from Selective Service again.

Jeff's plan was a little different. When his name was called, he didn't respond. Someone walked through the waiting area yelling, "Jeffrey Johnson!"

"Oh, that's me," Jeff said. "Sorry." He pointed to his ears. "Hearing problem."

The doctor decided to give him a hearing test.

"Just hit this button as soon as you hear the tone," he said.

"Okay." Jeff had trouble not smirking. Each pitch got louder and louder, but Jeff didn't respond.

"Can you hear it now?" the doctor asked, raising his voice. Jeff shook his head. Suspicious, the doctor turned it up several notches.

Jeff pushed the button. "I heard that," he said. He acted excited.

The doctor stared at him. Jeff held his gaze and didn't flinch. "I'll be right back," he said to Jeff. When he came back, someone came up behind Jeff and whispered loudly, "Son, can you hear me?" Jeff just sat there. The doctor watched him closely.

"Son, can you hear me?" This time it was loud. Jeff didn't move.

"Hey! Can you hear me now?!"

Jeff casually turned around as if he faintly heard something. Finally, the examiner said, "Okay, you're a 4-F. You'd better get checked by a specialist."

"What?!" Jeff screamed.

He pointed to the door and motioned for Jeff to leave. Jeff got up and started walking out. The examiner called, "You forgot your wallet!" Jeff kept walking. He knew it was a trick. Once outside and a short distance from the office, they all celebrated their freedom from the draft.

Jeff and Karyn started dating, often taking river trips together, partying, and getting high. Jeff constantly talked about his search for truth and God and about all the books he read and tapes he listened to. One night they took a drive out into the desert. They sat in the car, talking.

"I listened to this one tape the other day," he said, "and I was hypnotized into a deep meditative state."

"You were hypnotized?" Karyn's voice was clearly skeptical.

"Yeah. He kept repeating things like be calm, be restful, now go toward the light, and receive peace."

Karyn rolled her eyes. "Yeah, okay. And then?"

"He said to take some deep breaths. Now you're relaxed. Now you have peace." He watched Karyn's reaction. She obviously wasn't that interested. "Then it was so cool," he continued. "I was so relaxed that my hand slowly raised to my forehead just like he suggested on the tape." He looked at her. "Can you believe it?"

Jeff at the Colorado River, 1969.

"And this helped you?" she asked with unwelcome frankness.

"You think all this is stupid, don't you?" Disappointed, he said, "Well, so does my dad. When he hears me talking to my mom about any of this, he just leaves the room." He stepped out of the car and looked up at the sky. "Where is God?!" he screamed at the stars. "Where are You?" Silence greeted him.

Karyn walked over and put her arms around him. "Who cares where God is?" she answered. "Let's make out." She touched her lips to his.

Jeff's mother kept encouraging Jeff to go to college, and he finally decided to give it a try. He took a police science course at Cerritos College, but only lasted a few months.

High every day, he had trouble focusing in class. He thought it would be cool to be a cop, wear a badge, and have all that authority. He didn't realize how much studying was involved. The Law; the Justice System—it was too overwhelming. He couldn't cut it. He dropped out.

Jeff and Doug decided to get an apartment together. Jeff got a job at the local soap factory, but he didn't earn enough to cover expenses. He increased his drug pushing to bring in more money. Drug parties were a regular routine. One night Karyn and a group of friends were over. As everyone got high, the music was turned up a few notches. Finally, a neighbor called the police.

They pounded on the door and Jeff let them in.

"Having a party?" It was a comment, not a question. "We got a complaint from one of your neighbors."

"Sorry," Jeff said. "We'll turn the music down."

"Are there any illegal drugs on the premises?" It was obvious that everyone was high.

"I don't know what you're talking about, man." He said this with a slight smile of defiance on his face. Then he and his friends sat in the lotus position.

"We'll find it," one officer said. Making their way through the apartment, they searched for drugs and found one acid tab and some seeds. The arresting officer turned to Jeff and held up the evidence, "This could put you away for a while."

"Never saw it before," Jeff said in an arrogant tone.

"Oh, really?" The officer slammed Jeff up against the wall and snapped handcuffs around his wrists. "We'll put that in our report." He glared at Jeff. "You're going to jail."

"Everyone line up here," one of the other officers commanded. He took out his handcuffs.

"Please," Karyn begged, "don't handcuff me." She fought back the tears and was filled with humiliation. "That's not necessary. Just bring me down."

The whole group was taken to jail. Most made calls home to their parents and were released on bail. Karyn was also set free, but Jeff and a few others were held for several days.

Jeff and Doug decided it was too expensive to keep the apartment, so Jeff moved back home with his parents. He and Karyn continued to date, and Jeff got more and more into different philosophies and yoga.

"I don't know if you're more interested in the philosophy or in the new source of drugs," Karyn said one day. "I heard Paul say he got LSD directly from the Martinez brothers, Leary's right-hand men."

"It's all part of the package," Jeff said. "Part of the search for higher reality."

"Well, I have to face my own reality," Karyn said. "I'm going to start nurses' training. I found a work program where I can earn some money while I study."

"I don't know what's next for me," Jeff admitted. "I just know there must be something more out there." He stopped and looked at Karyn's face. She was pale. "You don't look so good. Are you okay?"

"Yeah, I just got a little touch of the flu or something." She had lost some weight and appeared tired.

A short time later Jeff received a phone call from Doug. He had gone to Hawaii and wanted Jeff to join him.

"I'm going to Hawaii," Jeff said to Karyn.

"Why?"

"Because I think I might find God over there." Then he added, "Why don't you come too?"

"No, I can't," she said.

"Why not?" He swung her into the circle of his arms and said, "Come on, babe. Come with me."

"I'm already enrolled in school, I can't just drop everything and go to Hawaii." There was a sourness in the pit of her stomach.

"I'm leaving tomorrow," he said. "I'm going to miss you."

"How long are you going to be gone?"

"Don't know."

"I hope you find whatever it is you're looking for." A heaviness settled in her chest. She wanted to say more, but couldn't. After he left the house, Karyn closed the door and leaned against it. She felt the tears rise in her eyes. She stood in lonely silence, wondering if she should have told him. The tears overflowed and slid down her cheeks. She was pregnant.

Chapter

11

The American Dream Gone Sour

Jeff's trip to Hawaii did not turn out as he expected. The surfing, LSD trips, yoga, self-realization, Jimi Hendrix concert, and other experiences left him still feeling unfulfilled and disillusioned. He moved back home with his parents and promised he would get a job. He called a few friends to tell them he was back in town, then he drove to Karyn's house.

While Jeff was in Hawaii, Karyn wrote a few times and had even sent him some money. But she never told him that she was pregnant. Her dream was to marry someone really in love with her, not someone who felt obligated because of a pregnancy.

She didn't even tell her parents until she realized she couldn't hide it anymore. One day she and her mom were shopping for a baby gift for Robyn, her brother Rusty's wife. When they got back to the house, Karyn told her mother that she was keeping the gift she bought.

"This is for me," she said. "I'm pregnant."

Her mother couldn't speak for a moment. "What are you going to do?"

"I'm going to keep the baby," she said firmly. "If this embarrasses you and you want me to move out, I'll move out."

The whole conversation with her parents was awkward and difficult. But they got through it and insisted she stay at the house with them. She was now seven months pregnant.

Jeff knocked on her front door. He adjusted his bell-bottom jeans and fingered the beads hanging over his linen shirt with long, flowing sleeves. His hair was long, his beard thick. He really looked forward to seeing Karyn again. She was a very attractive young woman who always took good care of herself. She was slender and in great shape.

"Hi," Karyn said brightly as she opened the front door. "Welcome back."

"*Aloha*," Jeff said, as he immediately noticed her stomach. He stood there for a moment in shock, staring at her. He finally managed to speak. "You're pregnant? Wow." He sat on the floor, legs crossed in a lotus position. "Why didn't you tell me?"

"I didn't want you to feel ... I mean, I'm handling it just fine by myself." She thought of all the tears, the sleepless nights. There was no point in bringing all that up. She quickly changed the subject. "So tell me about Hawaii."

"Man, it's the coolest place." His face lit up as he talked about the blue water, the surf, the many experiences he had there. Now that it was behind him, he forgot many of the negatives. He didn't mention eating only rice and bananas or being broke most of the time and almost dying in the jungle.

"You sound like a guru back from a Himalayan experience," Karyn said. "Did you find what you were looking for?"

"I don't know. I guess not," Jeff sighed. "There's got to be something more." He got up off the floor and sat next to her. "I really care about you," he said, putting his arms around her. "I want to spend more time with you."

They saw each other almost daily and their relationship grew closer than it had ever been. Jeff spent time with his druggie friends as well, but Karyn didn't want any part of drugs or alcohol while she was pregnant. When it got close to the baby's due date, Jeff took her to the zoo.

"I heard somewhere that if you do a lot of walking and exercise, you can help labor to start," Jeff said. He pushed her to walk fast and to climb up a birdcage display.

"I'm exhausted," she complained. "I know I'm big and uncomfortable, but this is getting ridiculous." She patted her stomach. "I think I need to go home," she said. "I don't feel so good."

Jeff brought her home, and when she told her mother how she felt, her mother said, "You're in labor."

Jeff got her into the car and drove her to the hospital.

"Hurry!" Karyn said. "Ooooh ..." She groaned in pain.

"Hang on, we're almost there." He screeched into the emergency room parking lot. "Wow, walking around the zoo worked," he said. "Boy, that was easy."

"Easy?" Her voice rose an octave. "Easy? You should feel what I'm feeling right now!"

Within minutes of arrival, Karyn delivered a baby girl. She named her Christina Lynn. When everything settled down and Karyn was brought to a room, Jeff came in and held her hand. "She's beautiful," he choked out. "I really do love you, Karyn. And I want to marry you."

When Karyn went home to her parents with the baby, she started planning the wedding. They decided to wait until Christy was two months old and Karyn got her energy back. Her parents liked Jeff, and they were happy about the wedding.

"Jeff brings sunshine into the house," her mother said. "Unlike some of your past boyfriends," she added.

They decided to have the ceremony in one of the local churches and began to check them out. One pastor insisted on a premarital counseling session. Jeff thought it might be interesting to discuss philosophy with him, so he went along with it.

At first, the pastor asked some basic questions. But as the discussion came to a close, the pastor asked Jeff a twisted, overtly sexual question that floored him. The pastor cleared his throat and waited for Jeff's reply.

Stunned, Jeff didn't know what to say, so he didn't answer. His face reflected his shock. The pastor awkwardly announced that the session was over.

"That guy's a pervert!" Jeff said to Karyn later. "He's the one who needs counseling."

"He's disgusting," she said.

They found another church.

On their wedding day, Karyn received a phone call from her old boyfriend. He had been declared missing in action in Vietnam, and she assumed he was dead. Now his voice came over the phone like a ghost from the past.

"Karyn, I'm back. I'm coming over to see you." There was no response. "Karyn? Are you there?"

"Yes," she stammered. Her emotions rushed through her like a roller coaster. "But this isn't a good time."

"How about tonight?"

"Uh, no. Tonight is definitely not good."

"What's going on? Don't you want to see me? After all I've been through?" Irritation crept into his voice.

"I'm getting married today," she blurted out. She hung up the phone, trembling. "This is crazy," she said to herself. "What timing."

"Karyn," her mother said, interrupting her thoughts. "Are you ready to go?"

"Yes, I'm ready."

"Who was that on the phone?"

"Nobody ... an old friend." She gathered up her things and said, "Let's go."

Jeff bought beads and rosaries for the men in the wedding party.

"What are you doing with those things on?" the pastor whispered to Jeff.

"Hey, it's for God, man." Jeff gave him a look that said, "Back off."

Jeff and Karyn on their wedding day, April 26, 1969.

After the ceremony, everyone was invited to Jeff's parents' house. The liquor flowed, and it didn't take long for most of their friends and many of the adults to get smashed. Jeff and Karyn left the party late and drove to Long Beach. By the time they got to their room, they both passed out drunk. The next morning they flew to Catalina, known as the poor man's Hawaii, for their honeymoon.

As the small plane descended, Jeff, now high on drugs again, shouted, "We're going to crash!"

"We're not going to crash," Karyn said. "What's wrong with you?"

"Look!" Jeff said, pointing out the window. "We're diving straight into the water. We're crashing." He put his head down and covered it with his hands.

"We're on a pontoon plane," she said, laughing. "We're supposed to land on the water."

After a brief honeymoon, reality set in and Jeff had to get a job. His dad got him work as a welder's apprentice.

Karyn's nurses' class, 1970.

He was installing dry cleaning equipment, which paid pretty well. Karyn entered a work / study program at the hospital with the goal of becoming a licensed nurse, and a baby-sitter took care of Christina. They rented a little house with a white picket fence. For a short while, Jeff stayed away from drugs. Things were going well. He began to think that maybe this was part of what he had been missing—a house, a wife, and a baby—the American dream.

He continued his search for truth, reading about different religious practices and talking to people. He made a shrine in a corner of the living room, with photos of different gurus, a picture of Jesus, and another of Paramahansa Yogananda. A tapestry hung on the wall, and candles and incense burned whenever they were home. Religious beads lay on the table around the candles.

"This is all very weird," Karyn complained one day when she came home from work. "I never know when I come home who the 'lord of the week' is." She kicked off her white nurses' shoes. "I'm embarrassed when my friends come over."

"Your friends?" His tone became sarcastic. "I don't see any of them seeking a higher plane, so who cares what they think?"

One day some Jehovah's Witnesses came to the door, and Jeff invited them inside. They glanced at his shrine in the corner and noticed the various meditation and metaphysical books lying around. Soon they were in a hot and heavy conversation. They said that taking blood into the body through the veins violates God's laws and invites His punishment.

"You mean they shouldn't be giving blood transfusions to people in the hospitals?" Jeff couldn't believe it. How many people would die if they followed that philosophy?

"Jehovah made the earth for a purpose," one of them said. "But because the first couple failed to fill the earth with righteous families who would care for His creation, the Bible tells us, 'The wage sin pays is death.'"

"Are you saying we're going to die because we're not taking good care of the earth?" Jeff asked.

"Only those who proclaim the good news of the kingdom, a flock of 144,000, will go to Heaven and rule."

"The earth will never be destroyed," another added, "but God will eliminate the present system of things in the battle at Armageddon. Hell is mankind's common grave."

Jeff got agitated with all the talk about hell. It scared him, and he told them to leave the house.

"What do you think about what they said?" he asked Karyn after they left.

"I used to hear all this rhetoric as a child from my grandfather," she said. "Who cares?" She continued to paint her nails. "Blah, blah, blah."

"Do you think there's any truth to what they said?"

"Like I said, who cares? It's all just a bunch of mumbo jumbo." She blew on her nails to dry the polish. "Believe whatever you want." She got up to leave the room. "I'm going to bed."

He sat up half the night thinking. The Mormons who came over based their beliefs on the experiences of a young teenage boy, Joseph Smith. He claimed that God and Jesus appeared personally to him, and later, angelic beings. They combined the Bible and the Book of Mormon and came up with their own set of beliefs.

"It's all so confusing," he thought. "Maybe there is no real truth."

They started going with Karyn's old friends on regular trips to Mexico, getting into the party scene, drinking lots of wine, and smoking marijuana. It didn't take much to get back into the old drug routine.

Jeff's friend, Paul, stopped by often and always had a supply available. He drove a brand new car and brought Karyn beautiful silk scarves and other gifts. He made several drug runs to India, and one day he brought Jeff some black opium.

"You've got to smoke this," Paul said. "It's the greatest stuff ever."

Jeff became hooked and couldn't go anywhere without it. He'd panic if his supply ran low. Every night he sat on the sofa, took a couple of strong hits with his hash pipe, and then passed out. Karyn would wake him up in the middle of the night and try to get him to come to bed. She tried to talk to him about it, but he wouldn't listen. One of Jeff's friends from Hawaii took a heavy dose of LSD, claimed he saw the pure light, then committed suicide. Jeff simply increased his drug use.

One night Karyn picked up his pipe and said with disgust in her voice, "You care more about this than you do about me." She put it down, "There's your religion. That pipe is sacred to you."

Jeff flew into a rage. "If you ever touch my drugs ..."

"You'll what?" Karyn said defiantly.

He bolted across the room and knuckled her upper arm where she had just received a shot at the hospital.

"Ow!" Tears instantly rose in her eyes, and she clutched her arm in pain. She glared at him and stomped off to the bedroom.

They began to argue and fight on a daily basis.

"You moved my stuff!" he shouted one night.

"What stuff?"

"I keep my books in the middle of the coffee table, just like this," he said, straightening them out. "And you moved the furniture."

"I did not."

"Look at this." He pointed to small, round indentations in the carpet.

"I vacuumed," she said. "Give me a break."

"Well, the furniture should be put back where it was so that you don't make more holes." He moved the chair a few inches back into its exact spot. "If I were a blind man, I'd want to know that my chair is right there." He sat down. That's when he noticed the shoes.

"Don't you start with my shoes," she warned him. "When I get home from the hospital, I'm tired. And if I want to kick them off right there and leave them, I will!" She snapped on the television, sat down on the sofa, and put her feet up on the coffee table.

"What do you think you're doing?" he asked.

"Relaxing. Watching TV. What does it look like I'm doing?"

"You haven't done the dishes yet. How can you sit down and watch TV?"

"You are driving me crazy!" She screamed at him, then she got up and went to the kitchen. Dishes, pots, and pans clanked in the sink. Christina started crying. "Now look what you've done," she yelled. "You woke up the baby."

Later, Jeff smoked his hash pipe while Karyn curled up on the opposite end of the sofa. She looked over at him and said, "You know, this isn't fun anymore." Tears flowed down her face. "I hate this. Is this all there is? Is this what marriage is all about?"

Jeff looked at her through glazed eyes. "I don't know," he said. Her white nurses' uniform was a blur. Then he passed out. Karyn went to bed. Sleep didn't come for a long time.

Chapter

12

I Found the Light

"Paul should be getting back soon," Jeff said to Karyn one night. He was worried about his low supply. Paul continued to smuggle drugs and supply Jeff, his friends, and others with whatever they wanted. He told Jeff that on this trip he would bring him back a big ball of black opium.

"I hope he's okay," Karyn said.

"He knows what he's doing." Jeff lit up his pipe. "He said this might be his last run. He's been buying hashish in India for one hundred dollars a pound and selling it here for one thousand dollars a pound. But he found out he can get the same stuff in Pakistan for ten dollars a pound. They call it 'black death.'" He shook his head. "That's an incredible profit."

"What he's doing is so dangerous," Karyn said. "He could end up in prison, or dead, over there."

Paul had connected with some guys in the Brotherhood out in Laguna who were part of Timothy Leary's group. One of them had arranged through his father, who worked for a major airline, to get Paul, himself, and another guy free tickets. With the help of someone in airline maintenance, Paul got on the plane well in advance, and with tools supplied to him, created a hidden compartment on the plane where they could stash their drugs on the way back and avoid customs. Their plan was to go through customs in Hawaii, while their drugs were stashed on the plane, then fly on the same plane to Los Angeles, pick up their stash, and be home free.

Paul knew he was pushing the edge of danger. He had spent some time in Europe preparing and planning this last big run. He flew to Pakistan and hooked up with his buddy, Chuck.

They took a taxi to the hotel, along with two other passengers. They whispered in the cab about where they would get the hashish. One of the other passengers said he could help them with that. They settled in the hotel, gave this guy some money, and waited. And waited. They knew something was wrong. Their connection finally came back and said he wanted more money. Fearing for their lives, they gave him what he asked for. In return, they were given three, 40-pound satchels of Pakistani hashish with gold seals on them. Peering out their hotel room window, they noticed a lot of military personnel roaming around outside. Afraid they might get busted, they removed a ceiling panel in the room where the air conditioner unit was, stuffed the bags up there, and re-sealed it.

They summoned a taxi to the airport, leaving the hashish at the hotel room for the moment, but taking their other luggage, just in case they were being watched. It was their dry run. Vehicles with machine guns mounted on them were everywhere. At the airport, they were told there were no flights out that night. They walked back outside to grab a taxi back to the hotel.

Men with black hoods covering their heads surrounded them and demanded that they open their luggage. One of the men removed his hood, and Paul recognized him as one of the passengers in the taxi. He flashed his ID. He was Chief of the Narcotics Division there in Pakistan. They searched the luggage, but only found dirty clothes. Angry, they had to release Paul and Chuck. Back at the hotel, they could see that their room had been searched.

"Check the air conditioner vent."

"Everything's still here," Chuck said.

106

Paul shook with fear. "I need something to calm me down."

They bought tranquilizers in the hotel pharmacy and went back to their room.

"I read in a newspaper that they arrested two Americans last week," Paul said. "This place is like a duck pond for shooting down drug dealers." His body shook with paralyzing fear. He crawled into bed and prayed, "God, if You're real, and if You get me out of here without getting killed or busted, I'll do whatever You want."

The next night they caught a flight out and decided to leave all the drugs in the ceiling of the hotel. This just wasn't worth dying for. They flew to India and made contact with their connection there, but he was so angry when he found out that they had gone to his competition in Pakistan that he kept their money and the drugs.

"I can't believe he ripped us off," Paul said. "We're going back with nothing."

He called a friend back home in California.

"We're so glad you're okay, Paul. We've been praying for you."

"What?" Paul couldn't believe his ears. How weird. He decided his friend must be high on something.

"Hey, when you get home, we're having a party out at the lake, and we're going water skiing. We want you to come."

When he got back, Paul went to the party, but it wasn't what he expected. He left a changed man, and he wanted to share what he discovered with his friend, Jeff.

Jeff and Karyn greeted Paul at their house, glad that he was back.

"Where is it?" Jeff asked. "My supply is getting low. I thought you'd be back before this, man." Jeff was stoned.

"I don't have anything for you," Paul said. "Not opium anyway."

"What do you mean you don't have anything?" Jeff panicked. "Do I have to find another supplier?"

"Let's sit down," Paul said. "Let me tell you what happened." He carried a Bible and set it down on the coffee table. First, he told them the whole story of how they almost got busted in Pakistan.

"Wow," Jeff said. "I'm glad you're okay, man."

"I'm more than okay." A big smile crossed his face. "Listen, you may think this is crazy, but hear me out." He shared with them how he met up with his other friends when he got back and they were all high on God. "They asked Jesus into their lives, got rid of their drugs, and everyone is going to Bible studies and meetings over at Calvary Chapel in Costa Mesa."

"You've got to be kidding," Jeff said. Then he thought about the drugs. "You mean you really don't have any opium for me?"

"Listen, man, this is it. This is the answer. I even got baptized."

"What's wrong with you?" Jeff said. "What are you, some kind of religious fanatic now?" He paced across the room. "A Jesus freak!" He looked at Paul. "That's it? You're trying to tell me that's the answer?"

"I'm telling you man," Paul said. "You've been searching for the truth, the light. Well, the truth isn't just a philosophy, it's a person. And the person is Jesus. He's the Light of the world."

Jeff stared at him. His friend, his drug supplier, was sitting there grinning and peaceful. "You're nuts."

"I'm serious, Jeff. What have you got to lose? You've tried everything else." He stood to his feet. "I want you guys to come somewhere with me."

"Right now?"

"Yeah, right now. There's a guy teaching a Bible study at a little church just down the street. He's cool, man. Just listen to what he has to say."

"No way."

"Come on," Paul said. It was obvious he wasn't going to let Jeff off easy. "Come with me. We'll walk over there together."

"Quit your begging," Jeff said. "Fine. We'll go." He looked at Karyn. "Get the baby and let's go."

"You're both nuts," she said. But she went along with them, carrying Christina.

Strains of music filled the chapel as they walked in and slipped into the back row. Jeff looked around, checking out the scene. People were smiling and happy, quietly singing a song. Many closed their eyes, faces uplifted.

"Thy lovingkindness is better than life ..." The music rose and fell as they sang in harmony, creating a quiet, peaceful mood. Jeff noticed those singing with upraised hands.

"That's weird," he whispered to Karyn. She nodded in agreement. The music soothed Christina to sleep.

A man with a long beard and long hair stood up and began to teach. Jeff thought, "at least he looks cool, not some stuffy straight guy." Maybe he actually had something to say. He read the story of Noah and the ark from the Bible, then referred to Jesus as our ark. Jeff didn't understand what he was saying.

"If there's anybody here who doesn't know Jesus in your heart, who doesn't understand what it means to accept the Lord, but wants to, I want you to raise your hand."

Jeff thought, "Man, I've tried everything, but not Jesus."

"If you've been searching and you've tried everything and nothing satisfies, then you need Jesus."

"What is this guy doing, reading my mind?"

"You're here and you've never asked Jesus into your heart. You've never given the Lord a chance." He looked around. "Raise your hand."

"Jesus in my heart. I've never tried that one." Jeff raised his hand. Karyn looked at him.

"Now, those of you who have raised your hand, please come forward. We invite you to the prayer room."

Jeff stood to go forward. Paul smiled.

Karyn whispered to Jeff, "What are you doing?"

"I'm going down there," he said, "to see what this is all about."

Paul followed Jeff into the prayer room, and they stood with about five others who had come forward. Jeff's eyes were completely bloodshot from smoking opium earlier, and he still felt stoned.

"It doesn't matter who you are or what you've done," the leader said. "God loves you. You are a person of value, and He has a special plan for your life. I'm not talking about joining a church or a denomination. I'm talking about a personal relationship with the Son of God. He can be your closest friend. Someone you can trust. Someone who loves you, no matter what."

Jeff could feel the love in the room.

"God wants to give you a fresh start." He reached out to the ones on each side of him. "Let's hold hands and repeat this prayer together," the leader said. Everyone quieted down. "Lord Jesus, forgive me, a sinner. Forgive my every sin, and come into my heart and life and be my Lord and my Savior. Give me the strength, Lord, to live daily for You. Give me the strength, Lord, to read Your Word, the Bible, to pray, to be the person You would have me to be. I love You and thank You. In Jesus' Name, Amen."

Jeff repeated the prayer, along with the others, line by line. As he prayed, he began to come down off the drugs. The moment he finished the prayer, his head felt clear. He felt different, like an inner battle was over. Peaceful.

"The Bible says if you prayed that prayer and meant it, you have become a new creation." He smiled. "You're born again and adopted into the family of God."

Jeff fought back the tears that wanted to surface. "What is this I'm feeling?" They gave him a modern version of the Bible, *Good News for Modern Man.* Karyn was waiting for him at the back of the church. She looked at him, then at Paul. "You're both weird," she said.

When they got home, Jeff went for his pipe and the opium he still had left. Karyn watched him, figuring she would have to drag him to bed in the middle of the night as usual. She put Christina to bed, and then went to use the bathroom. Jeff was in there flushing all of his drugs down the toilet. Pot, opium, all his rolling papers, everything. Some things he simply tossed into the trash.

"What are you doing?" she yelled. "Are you crazy?" She tried to snatch the marijuana from him, but it was too late. "That's like throwing money away," she said.

"I don't need this anymore," Jeff said. "I've finally found the light."

"You have really snapped now," Karyn said. "You are way out there."

"You need to do this too," he said.

"Do what? Throw drugs away?" She looked at the swirling water in the toilet bowl. "Looks like you've got that one covered."

"You need to be born again."

"What?" She sighed. "Listen, maybe this is good for you. I don't know. I did that born again stuff when I was a kid in the Baptist Church. I don't need anything else."

"But did you really accept Jesus into your heart?"

"Yeah, yeah. When I was about ten years old." She walked away. "Just leave me alone."

Jeff crawled into bed feeling totally peaceful. As he drifted off to sleep, he thought, "I can't wait to tell my mother and family about this." He knew they would be happy for him. He was wrong.

Chapter

13

Turn or Burn

The next morning Jeff got up early to read his Bible before going off to work. The words seemed to come alive for him and the stories touched his heart. That night he went to a prayer meeting and connected with some other guys who were going regularly to Costa Mesa for Bible study. Some man named Chuck Smith was the pastor. Everyone seemed to like him. Jeff said he'd go. When he told Karyn, she was surprised.

"You're going to Bible study?" She picked up his paperback Bible and flipped through it. He had been underlining things that meant something to him. "Are you supposed to mark up a Bible like this?" She tossed it back on the coffee table.

"It's great reading," Jeff said, picking it up. "Listen to this. Jesus said, 'I am the way, the truth, and the life.' This is it," he said. "This is the end of my search."

"Whatever," Karyn said. "I can't go with you. I have to stay home with the baby."

Jeff became addicted to reading the Bible and got more excited each day. He soaked up Pastor Chuck Smith's teachings. He liked his style of explaining the Bible verse-by-verse, chapter-by-chapter. Calvary Chapel had gained a reputation as "the hippie church." Chuck and his wife, Kay, opened their hearts to all the youth, and it didn't matter to them if they were longhaired, bare-footed hippies. Costa Mesa was about thirty miles away, but Jeff didn't mind the drive. Karyn still figured he was just on another one of his kicks and he'd get over it soon. But he didn't. Every night he went to either a prayer meeting or a Bible study.

"You're gone all the time," she complained. "At least when you took drugs, you were here." She looked at him. "Well, sort of here."

"Why don't you come with me?" Jeff asked. "Give it a chance. You'd like Calvary Chapel. The people there are really turned on."

She did go with him a few times, but didn't like it.

"They're a bunch of radicals," she said.

One time Jeff brought her to Melodyland Christian Center where Kathryn Kuhlman held a healing service. Karyn thought it was weird.

"I don't understand you," she said. "This new kick of yours is driving me crazy."

"It's not a kick," Jeff said, trying to hide his frustration. "I've been searching for the truth for years and now I've found it."

"Yeah, sure. You used to push drugs on people. Then you pushed yoga on people. But now you want me to believe you found the *real* truth."

"The difference is that I never understood the Bible before," Jeff said. "You have to be born again to understand spiritual things. I always considered Jesus to be one of the great teachers. But now I know that He's the Lord of lords, the King of kings. He's the one who can change lives."

Totally frustrated, Karyn snapped at him. "Well, you go ahead and save the world then. But quit trying to save me!"

Jeff prayed that Karyn would see the light, then he went to visit his parents.

"Hi, Mom!" Jeff said as he walked in the door. "I've got some great news."

"Oh? What's that?" his mother asked, taking in the smile and glow on his face.

"I've found the Lord."

"What are you on?" his father asked, as he came into the kitchen.

"I'm high on Jesus," Jeff said.

"Now he's into Jesus," his father muttered. He turned and left the room, shaking his head.

"Okay," his mother said, "Tell me more. What's going on?"

Jeff shared with her what had happened to him when he went forward at the church and prayed to ask Jesus into his heart.

"I'm telling you, Mom, you need to get right with the Lord. And you need to do it right now."

"I don't know, Jeff. With you, it's always something new. And each time you try to convince others of whatever it is you're into."

"But this is the real deal," he said. "This is a matter of life and death. Heaven or hell."

"What?" She controlled herself and dismissed him with, "I'll think about it. We'll talk again another time."

He got similar reactions from other family members.

"You act like you're better than your family," Karyn said. "Like you're the only one with the truth. They probably want to give you a frontal lobotomy."

Jeff went to a prayer meeting that night and asked everyone there to pray for his family. "They think I'm crazy," he said. "But that's okay. Let them watch me. They'll see this is it. This is the real deal."

Like a zealot, Jeff started going over to the Stonewood Mall with a bullhorn. He shouted, "Repent! Repent, or you're going to hell!" He felt like a modern day Jonah.

When Karyn heard about it, she said, "You're like an oil well without a cap, spewing out all over everyone." She mocked him. "'Repent, or you're going to hell!' What's with this 'turn or burn' campaign of yours?" She got up to leave the room. "Let it go."

Jeff met a lot of new Christians, many of whom had their own understanding of how you were supposed to live and act. Wanting to be open to whatever God had for him, Jeff took it all in, going to meetings and seminars, exposing himself to a wide variety of speakers. He got confused for a while, getting caught up in the emotion of the moment. Some preachers seemed to be forcing their own methods on their audiences, rather than allowing the Holy Spirit to do the work in people's hearts. Whenever he went back to Pastor Chuck Smith, he felt grounded again and peaceful.

One day Jeff and Doug talked about some of their old buddies who were still into the mystical teachings of Paramahansa Yogananda.

"Instead of just praying for them," Jeff said, "let's go up to Big Bear and talk to them."

Doug agreed and they headed for Big Bear. On the way up there, they stopped at a head shop where drug paraphernalia was sold, along with metaphysical books on the teachings of various gurus.

"Hey," Jeff said to the guy running the shop, "we'd like to talk with you." The man walked out from behind the counter and looked Jeff up and down. He was a broad-shouldered, muscular man with long hair, a full beard, and hard eyes. "Yeah?"

"We want to talk to you about Jesus."

He motioned to a doorway and said, "Go ahead to the back room. I'll be there in a minute."

Jeff and Doug walked through the doorway, which led up a flight of stairs. They stepped into a room that looked like a shrine. Guru photos hung on the walls, statues stood in the corners, candles and incense burned, and pillows were scattered around the floor for seating.

Another door opened and a small group of men slowly entered the room, seating themselves in a circle on the pillows. They were all imposing enough to have been bouncers in a bar. One of them pulled out a huge reefer, lit it, took a deep puff, then passed it to the next one in the circle. When it reached Jeff, he whispered a prayer, "What do I do now, Lord?"

"I'd like to share something with you," Jeff said. "We're here to tell you about Jesus." He held the reefer in his hand.

"Stop right there." It was a low, deep voice.

"I used to believe and do what you're doing," Jeff continued, ignoring the warning, "but now I found Jesus. He's the way ..."

"Shut up!" Again the deep voice, this time much louder.

Doug glanced at Jeff. The fear showed on his face. The man with the deep voice stood to his feet and walked over to Jeff. "This is a house of peace," he said. "You have no right to barge in here and push your stuff on us." His voice was hard and full of warning.

Jeff passed the reefer on to the next one in the circle, and slowly stood up. He tried to speak one more time. "I just wanted to share what happened to me," he said.

"Shut up and get out of here!" He got in Jeff's face.

Doug scrambled to his feet and said, "Let's go, man." They backed away and slipped out the door.

"Let's kick the dust off our feet and leave, just like the disciples did when the people wouldn't believe," Jeff said. They stood outside the building and prayed that somehow God would close the place down, get rid of it. "They call it a house of peace, but did you feel the dark oppression in there?"

"It was heavy, man." Doug was glad to be leaving the area.

They continued up the road to the cabin where their friends were staying. One of them was Mike Noonan, a surfer. They all sat around talking and sharing well into the night. Jeff challenged them to ask Jesus into their lives. Around two o'clock in the morning, they all prayed, then gathered up their self-realization notebooks and studies, their drugs and paraphernalia. They ripped the guru photos off the walls. One by one, they tossed them into the fireplace. The atmosphere in the room seemed to be lighter with each item that burned.

"Burn, baby, burn," someone said. "Hallelujah!"

"This is just like the Book of Acts in chapter nineteen, where they burned all their occult stuff," Jeff said.

The next day they heard that the head shop where Jeff and Doug prayed had burned down.

"Whoa ..." Doug said. "That's really heavy."

"I hope they don't think we did it!" Jeff said. They both burst out laughing. He couldn't wait to get to their prayer meeting and share everything that had happened. "Maybe this will convince Karyn," he thought. But when he shared with her, he got a different response.

"You've gone off the deep end," she said. "This is like some kind of cult thing."

When Jeff told some of his new friends what she had said, they told him, "She's trying to pull you down, man."

Then they quoted a Bible verse out of context to fit the situation. "If you love your wife more than the Lord and you're not willing to give up everything to follow Him, then you're not worthy of Him."

"Wow," Jeff said. "That's heavy."

When he went home that night, Karyn was waiting for him.

"I've been talking to a counselor," she said. "A psychiatrist. I want you to come to counseling with me. We can't go on like this."

Really wanting the marriage to work, Jeff agreed and they made an appointment. He carried his Bible with him everywhere he went, so he tucked it under his arm as they entered the psychiatrist's office. After a few preliminary questions and comments, he spoke directly to Jeff.

"Your wife tells me that you talk to God." His condescending tone revealed the fact that he thought this was definitely out of the ordinary.

"Yes, I do," Jeff answered. He smiled at him and placed his Bible on his lap.

"Oh, you do, do you?" There was that condescending voice again.

"Yes," Jeff said with great confidence. "And I talk to Satan too!"

Karyn put her hands over her face. Then she looked at the psychiatrist. "See what I have to put up with?"

"Yeah," Jeff continued, "I tell Satan to get out of my life. Jesus is in my heart now and I'm not going to allow Satan to bug me."

"He's worse than I imagined," he said to Karyn, as if Jeff wasn't even in the room.

"This is the Word of God," Jeff said, holding up his Bible. "And I believe it, understand it, and intend to obey it."

"He's definitely brainwashed," the psychiatrist said, ignoring Jeff. "He's not open to change. He's like a communist after reading Mao Tse-Tung's *Red Book*." He sighed. "I hate to say this, but I think you should leave him. Get a divorce."

One day, soon after the session, Jeff came home from work and Karyn had moved out, back to her parents' home with baby Christy. She filed for divorce.

1970s

Karyn, Christy, and Jeff
at summer camp, 1972.

The Johnson family, 1977.

Christy, Tara, and Jeff, 1975.

Christmas, 1974.

Jeff and Karyn at the Garden Tomb, 1976.

One of Jeff's first baptisms, 1974.

Jeff in 1978.

Jeff's parents' 50th anniversary, 1974.

New Life Fellowship, July 1975.

Chapter

14

Starting Over

Discouraged, Jeff gave up the house and temporarily moved back to his parents' home. He kept asking everyone to pray for Karyn.

"She's my wife, and Christy's my daughter. That will never change. No matter what." He believed God for a miracle.

He and his friend, Paul, hooked up with some young believers who wanted to start a Christian commune in the area. The Christian commune concept was gaining popularity at the time. Mansion Messiah had opened in Huntington Beach and Gospel Gulch opened in Newport.

"We'll call it the 'Philadelphia House,'" Jeff said. "The house of brotherly love."

"Now we just need to find a place," Paul added.

The head of Teen Challenge in Los Angeles heard that they were looking for a house and contacted them. He said that his family was moving, and he knew a couple of the guys from the Bible study group, so he offered to let them rent it.

"I know you have had a genuine experience with the Lord, and I'd love to have Christians renting the house," he told them.

The two-story, four-bedroom house sat on a back street close to Lakewood and Firestone in Downey. Six of them moved in together. Two girls took the bedroom downstairs and agreed to do the cooking and cleaning. Jeff, Paul, Chuck, and Doug took the upstairs dorm-style bedroom.

Chuck and Doug had jobs already, and Jeff and Paul went down to City Hall to be certified as street number painters. They would do a whole neighborhood, painting the house numbers on curbs, then go back and knock on doors, asking for a donation. They carried a letter from the city to show that they were certified to do this. Although there was no obligation for people to pay, Jeff and Paul told them that a few dollars was a customary donation. They also witnessed to the people when they asked for donations.

Every morning they had devotions together before going to work, and each night they had a Bible study and prayer meeting. One day Paul talked with a girl on the street and invited her to come to their Bible study. A Christian already, Terry came and brought some of her friends. Still new Christians themselves, Jeff and Paul felt unqualified to be teaching others. They asked Pastor Chuck Smith for his advice.

"What's the matter with you guys doing it?" Chuck asked. "You can handle it."

Jeff went back to his old high school and got permission to hand out flyers on campus during lunch break. He began talking with the students hanging out in the parking lot, telling them his story and how Jesus was changing his life. Soon they had up to fifty youth cramming into the house for Bible study every night. Jeff and Paul bought guitars and learned how to play just enough to strum along when they sang choruses. They alternated nights teaching the Bible, simply reading a chapter, then talking about it verse-by-verse. At the end, they asked if anyone wanted to receive Jesus or be baptized in the Holy Spirit. Each meeting, hands would go up all over the place. Before long, the house exploded with kids and activities. This caused a problem with some of the neighbors.

Jeff and the others in the house stood out with their hippie-style clothes, long hair, and beards. Some of the neighbors were convinced that they were part of some Manson-type cult. Police raids became a regular routine. They looked for drugs, but of course, never found any. Everyone in the house witnessed to the police whenever they showed up. The controversy continued and a newspaper reporter picked up on the story, writing about it in a local paper.

Indication of whether the way will be clear for six young men to continue their reported helping Downey young men and women, boys and girls to free themselves from drugs by substituting the principles of Christianity for reds, LSD and heroin, could be given at the city council meeting Tuesday morning.

Some of the men and women living on McCahill have expressed fear of some of the persons who go into the house with the open door to obtain help, noting their "hippie" appearance.

Southeast News article on the "House of Philadelphia," 1970.

... Two women ... planned to have a notary public draw up a petition ... asking that the young men be moved out on the basis that their "Christian House" is zoned R-1 ... and is in reality a "public meeting place." [4]

During all of this excitement and growth, Jeff kept calling Karyn, telling her he loved her and was praying for her. Sometimes she simply slammed the phone down after yelling at him not to call her. She and a friend rented an apartment on the beach together, and she got back into the party scene. But she felt unhappy and unfulfilled. Jeff

Karyn, Jeff, and Christy at Disneyland during their separation, 1970.

didn't give up. He'd call and tell her, "Jesus loves you. He wants to be Lord of your life." She didn't want to hear it. Month after month, he called. Sometimes she agreed to see him, but it always ended on a bad note. She even dated someone else for a while. Then this guy told her he was leaving and going to Hawaii to search for the deeper things in life. "Oh no, not you too?" she thought.

The Philadelphia House was exciting, but along with the big increase in numbers came problems. One guy they had allowed to stay there brought heroin into the house, and they had to throw him out. Jeff and Paul were the house elders, so they had to handle both the good and the bad. Paul began seriously dating Terry and eventually said he needed to leave the house and get a job and go to school. He knew Terry was meant to be his wife. Finally, they dissolved the house and everyone went in their own direction. The youth were encouraged to go to Calvary Chapel. Most did.

As Jeff gained more understanding of the teachings of the Bible, he realized he needed more discipline in his own life. After his first job with his dad, he worked as a pipe / steam fitter in the union with Karyn's father. He was faithful at work and started to save money so that he could pay cash for a car. On his lunch hour, he listened to Christian radio programs. He realized he had goofed off for too long. The union registered him for school at the Los Angeles Trade Tech where he attended two nights a week, studying a variety of subjects, including drafting, calculus, and trigonometry. He faithfully did his homework. Although it would take a number of years, he was determined to complete what he started. This time he'd graduate because he had earned it.

Karyn left the apartment on the beach and moved back home with her parents. On New Year's Eve, she finally agreed to see Jeff. He picked her up and they drove around for a while, talking.

"Where do you want to go?" Jeff asked.

"Well, it's New Year's Eve. Let's party," Karyn said. She looked over at Jeff when he didn't respond. "What do you want to do?"

"I was hoping we could go to a special New Year's Eve service at Melodyland," he said. "I know it'll be great," he added hopefully.

"You're kidding, right?" She could see that he wasn't. "I don't believe you!"

"Okay, okay," Jeff said, frustrated. "Look, I just want to be with you. You want to party? Then we'll party."

"It's New Year's Eve," she said. "A night to have fun, not go to church!" Her voice rose and Jeff could see this was going nowhere fast

"Fine," he said. "We'll find a party to go to." He pulled into a convenience store parking lot. Trying to control the frustration in his voice, he asked, "What do you want? Vodka? Wine? We'll just go for it. I don't want to fight with you anymore." His voice broke and he fought back the tears.

"Okay," she said, calming down. "I'm sorry. Let's just go to church." She started to cry.

"Karyn, I've missed you and Christy so much." Tears choked his voice. They sat in silence for a moment, both overcome by emotion. Then he pulled out of the parking lot and drove toward church. It was a beautiful service, and Jeff could see that it touched Karyn. They began to spend more time together and eventually, she went forward at a service, inviting Jesus into her heart. It was one of the happiest days of Jeff's life. Later, she was baptized, along with a friend of hers.

Jeff's parents, Christy, Karyn, and Jeff after their second wedding, May 10, 1971.

Jeff and Karyn both agreed that they needed counseling in order to get back together, but this time it would be Christian counseling. They spent six months seeing Keith Ritter, a marriage counselor at Calvary Chapel Costa Mesa, who helped them through many of their problems and differences. They knew God wanted them to get married again, and they planned their second wedding. Pastor Chuck Smith performed the ceremony at Calvary Chapel with both sets of parents present. Jeff smiled as he thought of the first time he had laid eyes on Pastor Chuck. He had wondered what he could possibly learn from this older, bald-headed guy. Now he was a spiritual father to him.

During the year of their separation, Jeff had continued to believe God would put his and Karyn's marriage back together. He had stored much of their furniture and household goods in his grandmother's garage. After one of their marriage counseling appointments, Jeff took Karyn to the garage and opened the door.

"See this? I always kept the faith that we would get back together in God's time."

Jeff, Karyn, and little Christy settled into a small house in Downey. Two months later, Karyn discovered she was pregnant. Throughout all this time, Jeff continued to pray for his mother and talked to her often about the Lord. He knew she couldn't deny the reality of what was happening in his life, especially after the wedding. Then he received a phone call from her that filled him with joy.

"I need to come over and tell you what happened," she said. She came to their house and tearfully told them of the inner turmoil and struggle she had been going through for some time.

"I could see that what has happened to you and Karyn is real," she said. "Today, I was out on a sales call and when the

Karyn at the beach on her wedding day.

woman opened the door, I burst into tears and told her I needed someone to talk to. It must have seemed so strange to her, but she invited me inside. As it turns out, she and her husband are involved with something called Teen Challenge."

Jeff smiled. "Yes, I know all about Teen Challenge."

"I told them about you and how I'm so confused," she continued. "I said I just didn't understand what was going on. They talked with me for a while and answered a lot of my questions. Then we got down on our knees together in their living room." She looked up at Jeff. "I invited the Lord into my heart." The tears splashed down her cheeks. Jeff blinked back his own tears and put his arms around her.

"Now I understand what you've been talking about," she said.

Chapter

15

The Call

Jeff felt that he should get involved in a local church, rather than driving the thirty miles or more to Costa Mesa four nights a week. He and Karyn had settled into their house on Puritan Street in Downey. He went to several churches before he found a pastor who received him in love. Jeff volunteered to teach a Bible study for the youth on Friday nights. He followed Chuck Smith's example of going through the books of the Bible verse-by-verse. Attendance increased week by week. He taught them to focus on outreach and serving others. They did special projects, like painting the church building inside and out, and reaching out to kids on the streets. Jeff loved studying and obeying the Word, then watching the results God brought about.

"Karyn," Jeff said one day, "I've been studying about finances and tithing, and I think we need to start giving ten percent of our income to the church." He showed her some of the verses he was reading.

"Fine," she said. "If that's what you feel we should do, then let's do it."

"Are you okay?" he asked her. "Having trouble with morning sickness?"

"Morning sickness? How about all-day sickness? I feel terrible. I wasn't this sick when I was pregnant with Christy."

"I'm sorry," he said.

Jeff's Friday night Bible study continued to grow and at first, the pastor was excited about Jeff being there and about the increased attendance. But Jeff began to become aware of the undercurrents in some of their conversations.

"Jeff, I really appreciate the fact that all these kids are going to your Friday night study, but you need to emphasize to them that they should also be attending my mid-week service on Wednesday nights."

Another time he said, "Some of the youth are questioning me on how the gifts of the Spirit should operate in the service. They said you're teaching something different."

"I'm only teaching what I understand from the Bible," Jeff said. "Nothing more, nothing less." He wondered how much to say to the pastor. He felt uncomfortable with the way certain people would always stand up in the Sunday service, give loud and emotional messages in tongues, and prophesy. He had no problem with those things happening in a small group or a special service, but he felt the way it was done at the Sunday service would only confuse visitors. In fact, he hadn't invited his parents to the church because he knew their reaction would not be positive. "We're each responsible before God for what we teach," Jeff said. "If this is a problem, I'll step down."

"You'll tell the youth to come to my study on Wednesday nights instead?"

"Sure."

After a few months, the youth pressured the pastor to have Jeff teach on Friday nights again. Jeff agreed to do it, but he soon sensed there would be ongoing friction between himself and the pastor. He didn't want to cause any division.

"I feel that the Lord is showing me that I should leave the church," Jeff finally said. "This isn't the place for me. God wants to do something new."

"What? You are a vital part of this church. How can you leave?" Anger surfaced in his voice. "You've become a strong arm of this church, and now you're leaving? This can't be of God!"

"I'm uncomfortable," Jeff said. "I need to do what I sense God is telling me."

"Well, you're wrong!" he shouted at Jeff. "You're going to find that it's tough out there to try and start something on your own." He tried to calm down. "Jeff, you shouldn't leave. You need to stay. You're going to cause a split in the church."

"No, I won't do that," Jeff said. "I'm telling the youth to stay at the church. I'm not trying to take people with me. I'm sorry," Jeff said. "I've got to go."

Back at home, Karyn said, "He's jealous because your group got so much bigger than his. That's got to be hard for him to deal with."

Jeff began a Friday night Bible study in their house. It grew quickly, and their living room was bursting at the seams. Karyn, who had just given birth to their second daughter, stayed in the bedroom with little Christy, baby Tara, and a few other children to keep them quiet and out of the way during the study. When Jeff wanted to go to Costa Mesa, she declined to go along most of the time because it was just too much trouble to pack up the girls or get a baby-sitter. Since she couldn't sit in on the study at their house, she started to go to her mother's on Friday nights. "If I have to suffer and be relegated to the bedroom, I might as well be at my mother's," she thought. "At least she makes good pie and we can visit." She began to feel spiritually dry. Jeff was so caught up in the excitement of the moment, he didn't really notice.

"I believe God is calling me to start a church," he said to Karyn one day. "A church for those who are tired of religion and tradition, a place where we can teach the Word with real freedom. A church like Calvary Chapel."

"You're not going to have it here in the house?" Panic filled her voice.

"No, I was thinking about starting out at Furman Park for the summer months."

It was the summer of 1973, and he started Sunday morning services outdoors in the park with a dozen people and a few children. One of the couples was John and Connie Looney. They had introduced themselves to Jeff and Karyn at a local restaurant one night when they noticed Jeff praying before a meal. They started attending Jeff's home Bible study, and then continued with him at Furman Park. Jeff taught from the Book of Jonah, about running *from* God versus running *toward* God. Within a few months, twenty families joined their fellowship.

Jeff teaching at Furman Park, first meeting place of CC Downey, 1973.

As fall approached, Jeff realized they needed to find a building to meet in before the rainy winter months arrived. He and his assistant, Mike, found a place on the corner of Downey and 4th Street, and they put up their first sign, calling the church New Life Fellowship. It was an old antique store with a small room for an office and another little room for a nursery. Within a short time, eighty people crammed into the small space, and Jeff had to hold two, then three morning services in order to accommodate everyone. The men of the church helped to enclose and paint a little shack in the back of the building, and they used that for the older kids' Sunday school room.

So many young couples with babies came to the church that they soon outgrew their little nursery. An old house across the street became available, so they rented it for the nursery. Jeff felt like he was in spiritual boot camp, learning how to be a pastor and a teacher, not just an evangelist.

"It seems like everything you touch turns to gold," Karyn said one day.

"What do you mean?"

"I think if you picked up a rock, it would get saved!"

Jeff laughed. "It's God, not me." Then he sniffed the air and asked, "What's that I smell? Did you bake a cake?"

"Yes, I did." She sounded mysterious.

"Well, where is it? Can I have a piece?" He poked around the kitchen. "Hey, this looks like a birthday cake." He looked at Karyn. "I didn't forget someone's birthday, did I?"

"Uh ... no." She quickly busied herself with washing dishes. "I just felt like baking, that's all." A tear slid down her cheek, but Jeff didn't notice. She wasn't ready to reveal her past. How would Jeff react? Her secret pain would remain just that—her secret.

Jeff outside of the first "official" CC Downey church building 1973.

During this time of growth, the pastor from the first church Jeff had attended left the area. People from that church approached Jeff about getting ordained in their denomination and merging his church with theirs. They wanted him back. Jeff said he would pray about it.

"God has called you to start your own ministry," one of Jeff's friends told him.

"You're right," Jeff said. "I just wanted to be sure that it was God closing the door and not me."

Although he didn't feel that was the direction for him to go, he realized that to be accepted by other pastors in the area, he needed to be ordained. In God's timing, he was invited by Pastor Chuck Smith to attend the Shepherd School at Calvary Chapel Costa Mesa, where he was officially ordained. When he came back, he changed the church sign to Calvary Chapel of Downey.

Steve and Linda Todd joined the fellowship, Steve leading worship and Linda teaching Sunday school. Mike Sasso heard about the church through Calvary Chapel in Costa Mesa and started attending. Mike was engaged at the time, and his future wife was not interested in having their wedding in a little cracker box building with cockroaches running around. They attended another church for a while, but ended up coming back.

"The Italian stallion is back!" Jeff said, grinning, when Mike came to a Sunday morning service.

"I like coming here," he said to Jeff, "because I know if I bring unsaved friends, they'll be challenged and have an opportunity to accept the Lord." He looked at Jeff, with his bushy hair and beard, and smiled. "These hippies think of Jesus as anti-establishment. 'Abandon everything and follow Me.' They don't play games. The right ingredients for a revival."

When on his job as a pipe / steam fitter, Jeff felt frustrated. "I should be out serving God, witnessing. What am I doing here, wasting my time welding?" He knew it would mean a big cut in pay, but perhaps it was time for him to step into full-time ministry. He spoke to the elders, and based on the church budget, they said they could pay him only one-third of what he was earning.

"That's okay," Jeff said. "Somehow things will work out. Pastor Chuck always says, 'When God guides, He provides.'" He went home and told Karyn.

"Are you crazy?" Karyn asked. "How are we going to survive on one hundred dollars a week? Why didn't you talk with me before making that decision?"

Jeff's parents and Karyn's parents all questioned his sanity.

"You made it through five years of trade school, and now it's wasted."

"How are you going to support your family?"

Jeff stubbornly forged ahead, and the church grew even more with his full-time attention. But about three months later, the elders showed up at his house. They showed him the treasurer's report.

"We're struggling to pay the rent and the electric bills," one said.

"Even though the church is growing, there are a lot of young people who don't have much money and aren't big givers."

"What are you saying?" Jeff asked. "That I need to go back to my job?"

"Maybe you got ahead of God's timing on this, Jeff."

Later that night, Jeff prayed and paced the floor. "What do You want me to do, Lord?" He felt convicted and knew he had to keep a good attitude about work. He went back to work as a welder. The church grew even more and Jeff got busier than ever with weddings, funerals, counseling, and lots of other activities. Six months later, the elders announced there was enough cash flow to pay him full-time. This time he quit his job with everyone's blessing.

For missions outreach, Jeff and some others from the church went down to Mexico. They loaded up two vans with clothes, toys, and food. When they reached the border, two officials stood guard at the checkpoint.

"I heard they steal a lot of things people try to bring in," one of the men said as they slowed the van down to a crawl.

"Hit the gas!" Jeff suddenly shouted. "Just drive on through! They're not taking this stuff from us."

They raced through the checkpoint, and fortunately, no one came after them. Hearts pounding, praising God for their protection, they drove sixty miles into the desert of Mexico and came to a small village where the people lived in shacks made out of sticks and cardboard. It was dark outside when they pulled to a stop.

"Let's make a campfire to let the people know we're here on a friendly mission." They found an old tire and some sticks and set them on fire. Kids came scrambling out of their cardboard huts. Jeff and the others started playing games with them, using their limited Spanish. Soon the children were laughing and squealing with delight. Slowly the adults wandered over to see what was going on.

"We have some clothes and toys and food for you," Jeff said while one of the men interpreted. "But listen. All this stuff is going to be gone in a few months. It doesn't last." He looked around at the faces staring back at him in the firelight. "But we do have something to give you that is lasting. I want to share Jesus with you. Jesus loves you. *'Jesus te ama mucho.'*"

At the end of his short message, a woman walked up to Jeff carrying her little baby. It had a serious infection of some kind and its little face was all swollen on one side. The mother was short, so she lifted the baby up high in front of Jeff. It moved him deeply.

"Let's pray," he said to the others with him. They gathered around, laid hands on the baby, and prayed for healing. The woman gasped.

"Mi bebe! Mi bebe! Mi bebe fue sanado! Gracias a Dios!"

The whole village buzzed with the news of the baby's healing, and the people came out to see and hear Jeff. Many came to the Lord. They left Spanish Bibles for the people and promised to come back as soon as they were able. Jeff and the others who came rejoiced and sang all the way back home, especially when they passed through the border security checkpoint.

Karyn often teased Jeff and called him "the Bible answer man." He loved to study. One day, someone from the church asked him a question.

"Are demons real?"

Jeff was about to find out. Not just from the Bible, but from firsthand experience.

Chapter

16

Casting Out Demons

After two years, the church on the corner of Downey and 4th Street proved to be too small. The building held eighty people at each of the three services, and it was overflowing. Jeff and his assistant, Mike, began to search for a facility that would seat three hundred people.

"I heard the fire station in Downey is for sale," Mike said. They went and checked it out and came very close to signing an agreement, but it didn't quite feel right.

"Honda has two buildings available on Firestone," Mike said. "I think there's enough space for growth there and the location is good." The elders discussed it and agreed that they should put down a five hundred dollar deposit to hold it.

Jeff went there one day, walking around, praying. The building smelled like oil and grease, with stained cement floors. He just couldn't see having children and a nursery in there without major changes. He asked for their five hundred dollar deposit back.

"Why did you do that without talking with us?" one of the elders asked.

"I really feel that it isn't the right place," Jeff said.

"But we're bursting at the seams. We need to do something soon."

"When God shuts a door, He opens another one," Jeff said.

Within a month, they found a better location. During the summer of 1975, they moved into a former state tax building on Firestone Boulevard, a three-thousand-square-foot facility that held three hundred people in the main meeting room. It also had a couple of offices, a kitchen, even space to open a bookstore. Parking space was not a problem, and they received permission from the Montessori School behind them to use some of their space for Sunday school classes and a nursery.

With the excitement of a new location and continued growth in numbers, the church really started coming together as a family of believers. It was a very young group with lots of children. Children's ministry became a priority.

CC Downey's second church building, 1975.

Additional ministries began to unfold as members used their gifts and talents to further the work of the church.

Glenn and Peggy Kravig were newlyweds who had moved to Downey and had been under Chuck Smith's teaching in Costa Mesa. They did the convalescent ministry, visiting people in hospitals and nursing homes. They also held a Bible study in their home as part of the small home groups that Jeff formed to maintain the feeling of family and to meet individual needs in spite of the accelerated growth they were experiencing. He didn't want people to get lost in the crowd. The Kravigs initiated family picnics and hosted camping trips and baptismal gatherings, all of which helped everyone to get to know each other on a more personal level.

Within a year, Jeff had to hold two Sunday morning services, a Sunday evening service, and a Wednesday evening service. He met weekly for prayer and teaching with his board and leaders. In the midst of all this, he had the responsibility to be in close touch with those overseeing the Sunday school, the bookstore, the home groups, various outreach ministries, and counseling. Finances allowed him to hire secretarial help, but it felt like a whirlwind that he couldn't control. He just tried to keep up with the powerful flow of what God was doing in their midst. He reminded himself daily that it was God's ministry, not his.

He kept in touch with Pastor Chuck Smith through all of this, looking to him for guidance. Jeff and Karyn were invited to attend Calvary Chapel's pastors' conferences, along with a dozen other young couples who had started Calvary Chapels in California.

It was exciting for them to hear how the Holy Spirit was bringing people to the Lord and increasing the numbers at all the Calvary Chapels, giving them a common vision. Jeff soaked up the teachings of Chuck Smith, L.E. Romaine, Mike MacIntosh, Keith Ritter, and others. They spent hours in prayer together, listening to the voice of the Holy Spirit. Kay Smith spent personal time with the wives. Chuck and Kay laid hands on the pastors, dedicating them to their calling. It was a time of real bonding of friendships and an anointing of increased passion for ministry.

"'Thou therefore, my son, be strong in the grace that is in Christ Jesus. And the things that thou hast heard of me among many witnesses, the same commit thou to faithful men, who shall be able to teach others also. Thou therefore endure hardness, as a good soldier of Jesus Christ.' That's II Timothy, chapter two, verses one to three," Chuck said.

"Just remember," he continued, "there is only one person who can say, 'My church.' And that is Jesus. It's His church. You can't join it. You've got to be born into it." He looked into the faces of the couples present. "The church exists to bring glory to God and for the edifying and the building up of the saints, to bring them into full maturity so that they will engage in the work of the ministry, according to the gifts God has given them. So don't try to do it all yourself."

One of the couples Jeff and Karyn stayed in touch with was Raul and Sharon Ries. God had transformed Raul's life, taking him from rage and violence to inner peace. A martial arts champion with a black belt, he held kung fu classes as part of his ministry.

While at one of these pastors' conferences, someone rushed into the room out of breath, shouting, "There's a pastor who has a community church nearby. He needs help." He tried to catch his breath. "And he needs it now!"

Without hesitation, Jeff, Raul Ries, Mike MacIntosh, Greg Laurie, and a few others jumped in a car and drove to the church. Flashing lights, police cars, and fire trucks were everywhere.

"Wow," Jeff said. "This must be serious."

They scrambled out of the car and into the church, looking for the pastor's office. They stopped short in the doorway. The room was totally trashed. Bookshelves were tipped over and books and papers were scattered all over the room. Then they heard a commotion coming from the sanctuary and headed in that direction.

"The woman is in there!" someone shouted.

"A woman? What's going on here?" Jeff wondered. He and the others entered the sanctuary and saw a petite, slender woman standing near the front. They slowly walked towards her. Jeff noticed her eyes. She looked wild.

"We're here to help you," he said in a calm voice. "We just want to talk with you."

Mike MacIntosh was out in front, and as he got closer, the woman rushed him and kicked him, sending him tumbling to the floor. When Jeff and Raul tried to approach

144

her, she lifted them up in the air and tossed them around as if it was nothing to her.

"Don't you touch me," she shouted in a deep, evil voice. It ran shivers up their spines.

"She's demon possessed!" Jeff said. He had never seen anything like this before.

All three men tried tackling her together, but she had supernatural strength and flipped them around as if they were rag dolls.

"Take her down!" Jeff shouted to Raul. "You can do it!"

"Hey man, I'm trying! I'm trying!" He flipped through the air again, landing with a thud on the floor.

Finally, two more men joined them. Unbelievably, she managed to lift and fight all of them. Eventually, they got her down on the floor and began ordering the demons to come out of her in Jesus' Name. Her lips twisted into a cynical smile. Icy contempt flashed in her eyes. The intense steely edge of the guttural voice that came from this seemingly frail woman was frightening. They took authority, quoted Scriptures, and prayed over her. They knew the power of Jesus was greater than anything inside this woman.

"Greater is He who is in me than He who is in the world," Jeff said. For three hours, the men struggled with her. At one point Jeff went outside to get two of the police officers.

"Are you guys Christians?" he asked them.

"Yeah," they both answered.

"Then come with me. You've got to see this. It's something we don't see much of here in the United States. It's a case of authentic demon possession."

They glanced at each other, hesitated, but then followed Jeff inside. When they saw her wild eyes and heard her deep voice, they froze. She reared up and almost freed herself with her incredible strength. The officers turned on their heels. They wanted no part of it. By this time, Kay Smith and Jeff's wife, Karyn, had joined them to help in any way they could.

Finally, the demons left, the woman was exhausted, but peaceful, and they prayed with her to accept the Lord. They released her and she sat up with a beautiful smile on her face.

"What's going on in here?" Pastor Chuck Smith had just arrived on the scene. He looked around at the mess, at the overturned pews, and at the wiped-out pastors.

"You wouldn't believe what's been happening here!" Jeff exclaimed.

"Whoa," Raul said, sweating, his shirt torn. "That was something else, man."

They told Chuck about the demons, the woman's strength—the whole story.

"Well, has she received the Lord?" he asked calmly.

"Yes, she just prayed to receive the Lord."

"Good," Chuck said. He walked over to the woman and said, "Welcome to the family of God! What you need to do now, sister, is read your Bible and pray every day." He spoke to her for a few minutes about getting grounded in the Word and attending a Spirit-filled church. Then he left.

"Hey, how come he gets the easy part?" Raul asked. "Look at us, man. We're wiped out!"

They spoke with the woman's husband afterwards and found out that she had belonged to a witches' coven that had done many things, including sacrificing babies. He had brought her to psychologists and psychiatrists, and she had been examined and studied by medical doctors. But no one had been able to help her, until now. Jesus had set her free.

146

Jeff told his church later, "One of Satan's greatest ploys is that many deny his existence. People think of him as just a guy carrying a pitchfork, wearing a little red suit with horns, sporting a pointed tail. Because of this, he can be the serpent that he is, coiling himself around people, choking the life out of them." He opened his Bible to II Corinthians 4:4 and quoted,

> ... In whom the god of this world hath blinded the minds of them which believe not, lest the light of the glorious gospel of Christ, who is the image of God, should shine unto them.

Chuck and Kay asked Jeff and Karyn if they would like to go on a trip to Israel with them. Enough people had signed up to reserve two tour buses, and Chuck needed another pastor to oversee one of the buses. Jeff's parents agreed to watch Christy and Tara while they were gone. Jeff decided to have a special communion service at church the night before they left. His parents came to the service.

After he did a brief teaching, he said, "Now we're going to celebrate communion. If there's anyone here who doesn't know the Lord, just raise your hand, and I'll pray for you. Then you can take communion with us as part of the family of God."

Jeff's parents, 1974. Jeff's dad went home to be with the Lord in 1978, and Jeff's mom in 2000.

He looked around and saw a number of hands go up. But one hand in particular, way in

147

the back, caught his eye. It was his father. Jeff's eyes were moist as he prayed for him and the others. Later that night at the house, his father said to Karyn, "Well, I did it."

"What are you talking about? Did what?"

"I raised my hand in church tonight. I received Jesus."

Jeff and Karyn left on their trip the next morning with great joy in their hearts. They enjoyed Israel so much that the trip became an annual event, growing in number each year.

After the trip, Karyn was asked to be involved with an international women's ministry in their area, which resulted in her taking the position of vice president. Jeff went on six major outreach trips overseas that year in addition to all of his other conferences, activities, teaching, and responsibilities.

Karyn began to feel the weight of the load she was carrying. She was ministering to women at the church, continuing her involvement with another women's group, trying to live up to the image of being a pastor's wife, and being a mother to Christy and Tara. It was fast becoming more than she could bear. She tried to communicate her feelings with Jeff from time to time, but he was so caught up in the explosive growth and excitement of what was happening at the church that he didn't really hear her. He missed the symptoms of a home about to fall apart.

Chapter

17

Trouble at Home

The explosive growth at church continued, and when they reached nine hundred people after one year at the Firestone location, they had to begin looking again for another facility. Jeff thought back to the time just four years prior when he and several friends met weekly for prayer, pouring their hearts out for hours at a time for a church in Downey. They met in an underground shelter in an old house on Imperial Highway. At the time, it seemed that nothing was happening. Now he could see God's hand making things happen even more quickly than any of them had expected.

One day Jeff met with the accountant to review their finances. When they were finished, he leaned back in his chair and said to Jeff, "I believe I have a word from the Lord for you. It's about the church." He leaned forward. "You need to find a building that will hold fifteen hundred people!"

Jeff laughed aloud. "We're growing," he said, "but that's a bit much."

He left the office and drove down the freeway praying. "What are You doing, Lord? Is this true? Is the church going to continue to grow that fast? And where is there a big enough building in Downey to hold fifteen hundred people?" He drove around, continuing to pray. He reminded himself that, with God, all things are possible. Then he passed the Downey Civic Center. "The Civic Center? Would they even consider renting it for Sunday mornings?" He decided to stop in and ask.

"You wouldn't want to rent the Center to a church on Sunday mornings, would you?" Jeff asked. He felt sure the manager would laugh and tell him no.

"Hmmm, Sunday mornings?" He scratched his chin. "You know what? Let's talk about it. I think it could work." He got up from his desk and said, "Let's take a walk over to the auditorium."

As Jeff stepped up onto the stage and looked out over the rows of seats and the balcony, he thought, "Oh no, I can't do this, Lord. This is too big for me." Then he heard that still, small voice. "Yes, you're right. It's too big for you, but not for Me."

They talked about some of the details, then Jeff asked, "How many does it seat?"

"Seven hundred fifty."

"If we held two services, that's the fifteen hundred seating capacity we'll need. Wow." He drove home to tell Karyn about the prophecy and then to call the elders.

"Karyn!" he called, coming through the door. "I've got something to tell you." She didn't answer, so he went into the bedroom. She was lying down. "What's wrong? Are you sick?"

"Yeah, that's it. I'm sick." She closed her eyes, feeling utterly miserable.

"What's going on?" He sat on the edge of the bed.

"I was out grocery shopping and I heard someone whisper, 'That's Pastor Jeff's wife!' I wanted to scream, 'Leave me alone! I just want to get food for my family without someone checking me out.'" Tears sprang to her eyes. "Then I went to Sears to buy you some underwear. Someone in the check-out line recognized me, and I could tell they were checking out my purchases, probably wondering why I bought your underwear at Sears." The frustration tumbled out of her. She sat up.

"Then, to top it off, I get home and a couple was waiting on our front porch. They said they needed marriage counseling." She got up and started pacing the floor. "I wanted to scream at them, 'I don't want to hear about your problems! What about mine? How about if you listen to my problems instead?!'" Her heart pounded and she started trembling. "I feel dizzy," she said, crawling back into bed.

"Maybe you just need a rest," Jeff said. "You have been awfully busy lately." He hesitated, then said, "But you know, as the church grows, we're going to have to deal with these things. People recognize us out in public. So what?"

Karyn glared at him and muttered, "I knew you wouldn't understand."

"Do you want to hear my news?" She didn't answer, but he continued anyway, telling her about the accountant's prophecy and the possibility of renting the Downey Civic Center for Sunday services. He could hardly contain his excitement.

Karyn groaned and pulled the sheet over her head.

The church moved into the Civic Center, and within six months, they needed to go to two morning services to accommodate the growth. Jeff's schedule was more than full. Karyn's stress increased as she attempted to keep up with it all. She felt very lonely. One morning at breakfast, she confronted Jeff.

"Do you realize that you just got back last night from a two-week trip? And what did you do? You unpacked your suitcase and immediately went down to the church!"

"I had to check on things," he said defensively. "It's my responsibility."

"Your problem is that you don't delegate enough. You think you have to do everything yourself. Well, what about us? You have a family here."

"Karyn," Jeff said in a calm, but somewhat condescending tone, "You just need to spend more time in prayer, get your focus back on the Lord. Don't be like this. Get over it."

"What?!" She seethed with anger. She reached for the eggs she was about to cook for breakfast and hurled them across the kitchen at Jeff. They splattered all over him and the floor. Christy and Tara were sitting at the table. Their eyes widened and darted from Jeff to Karyn. They didn't know if they were next.

"Forget it," Karyn said. "Just go to church."

Jeff almost quoted an appropriate Bible verse, but then thought better of it. He changed his clothes and left for the office. Karyn cleaned up the mess, then showered and dressed for her women's meeting.

As she sat on the platform, waiting for her turn to speak, she glanced around at the other women on the Board. They all wore fashionable matching outfits and had stylish hairdos. Their nails were perfectly polished. She looked at her hands— no polish and a chipped nail. Her dress was long and flowing, definitely not the latest fashion. She did her own hair. Who had time to sit in a beauty shop? As she stood in front of the microphone, she suddenly began sweating, felt light-headed, and tightness in her chest filled her with panic. She looked out at the audience, all those eyes staring back at her. Suddenly, she burst into tears and dashed off the platform. Trembling, she called Jeff, and he came to pick her up.

"I feel like I'm having a nervous breakdown," she cried.

"This sounds like a spiritual problem," Jeff said. "It's the devil attacking because of all the great things happening in the ministry. We're going to come against this thing. You'll be fine." He prayed for her, and then went back to his office.

Karyn thought, "Maybe he's right. It's a spiritual problem. I know I'm not being a good pastor's wife." She lay in bed, staring at the ceiling, crying. "Or maybe he spends so much time at the church because the reality is that he doesn't really love me anymore and doesn't have the guts to tell me." Tears flooded her face. "Or maybe this is happening because I haven't told Jeff about ... No, I can't. I can't deal with that right now." Her secret past would have to remain unspoken.

Over the next year, she remained at home more and more. Negative thoughts swirled around in her mind. She went into a panic attack if she even thought about doing anything in public. She constantly made excuses for not participating in the many activities going on. Jeff got even busier with the church and spent little time at home. Depression overwhelmed her. Several times, she anonymously called a national ministry for prayer.

She got to the point where she didn't even want to walk outside to the mailbox. Fear gripped her. She didn't understand what was happening. She went for counseling a few times and was told by one psychologist that she was having panic attacks. "No kidding," she thought. She felt worthless. Her thoughts even became suicidal. That really scared her. Late one night Jeff was soaking in the bathtub and she went in to talk to him. Maybe this was the time.

"Jeff, there's something I have to tell you." Nervously, she moistened her dry lips.

"Okay," he said. "What?"

"I, uh ..." She could hardly lift her voice above a whisper. She cleared her throat. "Never mind," she said in a choked voice. "I can't tell you."

"What is it?" Jeff asked. A tinge of exasperation came into his voice. "Just tell me." He closed his eyes and tried to hide his frustration. She had come to him on a number of occasions as if she had some terrible secret. He had no idea what it was. What could be so terrible to hold her in such bondage? "Just tell me," he said again. When he opened his eyes, she was gone.

The next day Karyn asked Tara to pray at bedtime after reading her a Bible story.

"No!" she said defiantly.

Surprised, Karyn asked, "Why won't you pray?"

"Well, because I don't see God." She stared out into space. "And I don't see Daddy!"

When Jeff came home that night, after being away in the Middle East for two weeks, Karyn told him what Tara had said. Jeff felt stung. His ministry was thriving, but his family was crumbling. He agreed to go for counseling and to make it a priority. They went to Ron Wiseman, a Christian marriage counselor.

"I realize I've neglected my family," Jeff admitted. "I need to spend more time at home." He looked over at Karyn. "I will, I promise."

But the needs of ministry placed many demands on his time and although he tried, he still didn't spend quality time with Karyn and the girls.

"Jeff," Ron said in one of their sessions, "I want you to read Malachi chapter two. God is weary of your words, saying that you're sorry, that you'll change." He looked over at Karyn. "And Karyn is weary of them too." Tears bordered her eyes. He handed the Bible to Jeff. "Read the last part of verse fifteen."

"Therefore take heed to your spirit, and let none deal treacherously against the wife of his youth." Jeff's heart felt heavy. "Is that what I've done?"

"You tell me. Is it?"

"Yes, I guess I have." He felt a stab of conviction.

"Your family is your first ministry, your Jerusalem. You are the Lord's representative, first, in your home. You preach it, tell other couples about it, but you're failing to do it yourself," Ron said. "You need to repent and love your wife as Christ loves the church."

"It's not going to be easy," Jeff said, "with all the demands on my time."

"Do you know what your real problem is?" Ron asked. "You're having an affair. And the enemy is having a field day with your wife."

Karyn panicked, looking from Ron to Jeff.

"No, not an affair with a woman," Ron said. "You're having an affair with the church."

"Karyn, I'm so sorry." A heaviness settled in his chest. "I've been so insensitive to your needs. I can't believe I've been so blind. Please forgive me."

"And Karyn," Ron said, "You need to draw closer to the Lord and get more into the Word to receive the emotional healing that you need. It's okay to lean on Jeff, but your relationship with the Lord is *yours*. Nourish it."

Jeff changed his schedule to work out a balance with family and the infinite needs of the church. They set aside a weekly family night together. He started to realize how much Karyn did at home, keeping up with the house and the kids, let alone outside activities. He expressed his appreciation for those things. Karyn received further counsel about her panic attacks and was diagnosed with agoraphobia. Stress, anxiety, and fear were the foundations of it. She began to search the Scriptures concerning fear.

"For God hath not given us the spirit of fear; but of power, and of love, and of a sound mind." She repeated this verse from II Timothy 1:7 over and over. She really got into the Word, studying this and other topics. Excited about what she was learning, she decided to teach a women's Bible study at church. In spite of the anxiety, she took steps to face her fear of speaking in public. As she did, the fear lessened. And the women enjoyed and responded to her teaching.

Vacation times became a priority, and the family often went camping on the river with Karyn's brother Rusty and his wife Robyn. Their two daughters, Lisa and Tanya, got along well with Christy and Tara. Rusty enjoyed surfing and fishing with Jeff. Karyn loved camping because she enjoyed the outdoors.

"This is going to be great," Karyn said as she helped pack up for their camping trip. "The girls are excited too."

They set up their tents, ate their evening meal, and then Jeff and Rusty went fishing. Karyn and Robyn did the dishes while the girls played nearby.

"Wow, look at that sky," Karyn said. "It's so beautiful and peaceful out here."

Suddenly, a man armed with a sawed-off shotgun thrashed through the bushes and bolted right past them. Seconds later, the police dashed through their campsite, right behind him.

"Peaceful?" Robyn said. They both laughed.

When the men came back from fishing, they cleaned the fish for dinner, then stuck the fish heads on poles and in trees to attract wildlife during the night—coyotes, raccoons, wild mules, and birds of prey. They loved watching them. The women stayed close to the campfire and tents.

Each time they returned from their vacation, Jeff and Karyn felt so much more relaxed. Their marriage relationship grew stronger and they became one another's best friend.

The church continued to grow, and both morning services filled to capacity. They also began to run into problems with the Civic Center. Special events and major weekend theatre productions sometimes prevented them from using the building. On those Sundays, they met in the gymnasium of Downey High School. The acoustics there were poor, and Jeff felt bad for families who had to drop their children off two miles away for Sunday school, then go back to pick up their kids. The inconvenience was getting old.

"What building around here is bigger than the Civic Center?" Jeff asked.

They began to pray, asking God for help. A miracle was already in the making.

Chapter

18

Explosive Growth

Once Jeff faced his family problems, the church entered a period of explosive growth. After only one year at the Civic Center, they were desperately in need of a new facility. They held two Sunday morning services, and the attendance pushed fifteen hundred.

"God, You've got to do something!" Jeff prayed.

"Hey," one of Jeff's friends said, "Why don't you go over and take a look at the old White Front building?" He grinned. "It's the only one I can think of locally that's bigger than what we have now."

"Yeah, right," Jeff said.

White Front/flea market building, 1979.

The White Front store had filed for bankruptcy, leaving behind a vacant 150,000 square foot building on a twelve-acre lot. A portion of it was temporarily being used and advertised as the largest indoor flea market in the world. A gas station stood on one side of the property and there was a large market on the other side.

Jeff peered into the windows of the vacated market portion of the building and figured it was about thirty thousand square feet. "Perfect," he thought. "We could seat fifteen hundred in here easily." He made some inquiries and found out that Demos Shakarian, the president of the Full Gospel Businessmen's Fellowship International, owned the property. Jeff called him to set up a meeting.

"Let's have breakfast together," Demos said.

Jeff liked Demos immediately. He was a simple, good-natured man who treated everyone like a friend. But he was also a good businessman.

"I'm interested in leasing part of the vacated building," Jeff said. "We're bursting at the seams and need another place to meet." He went on to explain the growth of the church and what God was doing in their ministry. "I noticed that you're not using the market portion of the building, which is separate from the flea market. That would be perfect for us."

"No, I'm not interested in leasing it," Demos said. "I'm tired of leasing, and I'm getting out of that business. I leased it to White Front, and they went bankrupt. Now I've got to deal with it again. I want to sell it."

"How much are you asking?"

"Two-and-a-quarter million," Demos said.

"Wait a minute," Jeff said, grinning and reaching into his pockets. "Let's see how much I've got." He pulled out some change and plunked it on the table. "I guess that leaves us out."

Disappointed, Jeff reported back to the elders and continued to pray. Within the next few months, there was virtually no room for more people to come to church. He went back to Demos.

"Demos, you've got to pray about this. We need your building. I know God speaks to you. We've got to lease your building."

"No," Demos said. "You're going to buy it." He looked at Jeff squarely in the eyes and said, "I've already prayed and now it's time to move." He told him about two other offers he had received from parties that appeared to have the finances to close the deal, but he wanted Calvary Chapel of Downey to have it. "Let's find a way to do it," he said.

"God will have to do a major miracle," Jeff said.

"Let me tell you a story about this property," Demos continued. "I used to have cows on this land. One time they got a disease, and to keep it from spreading to other cows in the area, we were ordered to destroy the animals. I called a few Christian brothers to come over and pray with me over the cows and all the corrals." He smiled. "God healed them and they didn't have to be destroyed. God is good!" He looked Jeff full in the face. "I believe this land is to be yours," he said. "I've dedicated it to God and I want God's business to take place here."

"But I'm just a kid with no money and a bunch of people," Jeff said. "I don't know anything about loans, mortgages, or big finance."

"How old are you?"

"Thirty."

Demos smiled. "God is doing big things in your life." Getting back to business, he added, "Do you have a lawyer?"

"I know one in Costa Mesa," Jeff said. "Why?"

"Have him call my lawyer and talk about how this could all come together. If it's of the Lord, it will all work out."

"Okay," Jeff hesitated, and then added, "There's something I need to tell you." It was his turn to smile. "We've already walked around your land."

"You mean like Joshua marching around the city of Jericho?" Demos laughed. "Well, don't go blowing the trumpets yet! I don't want my building tumbling down."

At the weekly prayer meeting of the church board, Jeff said, "We need to put in an offer on the White Front building."

"We don't have money for that," Steve Todd said.

"What is he thinking now?" Mike Sasso wondered.

"I sense God wants us there," Jeff said. "And I'm well aware that it will take a major miracle to make it happen." He looked around at the leaders. "Let's watch the miracle unfold."

After much discussion and prayer, they all agreed. The lawyers started meeting to discuss creative financing for the purchase. One of the first of about fifty major miracles was the $100,000 required deposit. A local bank agreed to loan the down payment. With many meetings, lawyers, and lots of negotiating, the papers were finally signed, and Calvary Chapel of Downey took over the building.

Over the next few months, many volunteers from the church put in hundreds of hours of work, tearing down, and then assisting with renovating and building the south sanctuary to seat fifteen hundred people. They also built enough classrooms for Sunday school during the services, and they decided to start a Christian school during the week. They completed the 30,000 square feet and still had 120,000 square feet remaining. On Easter Sunday, 1978, their first service was held in the new building.

As the church continued its phenomenal growth, the needs and staff increased. They talked about leasing out the unused portion of the building. That's when a representative of a major department store called.

"Let's make a deal on this space," he said to Jeff. "We'll put one of our stores in here, and we'll cover the cost of expanding the parking structure to accommodate more cars. That's a win-win situation."

At first, the offer sounded like it might be from God. It would certainly bring in the extra funds to allow them to continue to renovate their own portion of the building and to pay down the mortgage. The church even went through the expense of putting in a special firewall, separating the sanctuary from the remainder of the building, in case they leased it out. They met several times, but then came the conflict.

"We understand you want to continue having your church services at your already scheduled times and that during the week, parents drop off the students early in the morning. You asked us to open at eleven o'clock in the morning in order to avoid any traffic and parking problems." His tone changed. "But after all, we'll be bringing you a good deal of money, and we've decided to open the store at nine o'clock in the morning."

Jeff leaned back and took a deep breath before he responded. "Which means your store employees and others will be arriving at the same time as the parents dropping off their children."

"That's right." His voice was almost defiant.

"There's something you need to understand," Jeff said. "The needs of the church come first. The needs of the Christian school come second." He looked him in the eye. "And you come last."

"But we'll be losing thousands of dollars by opening at eleven instead of nine."

"I'm sorry," Jeff said, standing to his feet. "This just is not going to work." His voice was firm, final.

"Do you realize the deal you're passing up here?" He spat out the words as he gathered his papers.

"What I know is that I don't have peace about it," Jeff said. "But thanks for the offer."

Later, it proved to be a wise decision, since they were going to need the use of the entire facility themselves. An article in the *Southeast News* during that time reported, "Storefront church is Downey's largest." The reporter questioned Jeff on the advertising budget for the church.

"Our advertising budget isn't $10 per month," he said. "We study the Bible and we sing. Pastors from other churches come here all the time and ask how we do it. They want to know what our 'program' is. We don't have a program. People are looking for substance. We're reaching them." [5]

A survey showed that about sixty percent of the congregation was made up of people between the ages of twenty-five and thirty-five, mostly young families. Another thirty percent were younger than twenty-five, and only ten percent were over thirty-five years old.

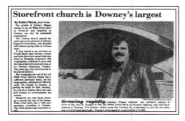

Southeast News article, 1980.

"Music and worship are a big part of the church, and that's one reason young people are attracted to it," Jeff said. "It speaks their language. They like the beat and they listen to the message."[6]

With so many young families, the registration of students at their Christian school continued to increase. Phil O'Malley, with a Master's Degree in business, became the school's principal early on. At a staff meeting one day, he said, "I used to teach in a public high school. Now I feel like I've gone to Heaven. I love these kids." He learned every student's name and sent each a Christmas card every year.

Not all the students appreciated the Christian environment. Some, like Louie Cruzado, rebelled. He was always in trouble, seemingly spending more time in the principal's office than in the classroom, so he chose to leave rather than be expelled. But the loving impact of the Christian atmosphere stayed with him, and later, he completed school, became the junior high pastor at the church, and married Tracy Sasso, the daughter of Jeff's assistant pastor.

Another student who had to be expelled for his behavior later started a Bible club and came back several times to speak at the school's chapel. He said that his experience at Calvary Chapel Christian School, with the teachers holding him to a high standard and not allowing him to manipulate them, had made a permanent impact on his life. He realized that he needed to get his act together, and now he was serving the Lord.

With the church established in their new White Front location and the school grounded and growing, Jeff got a visit from a Montebello police officer that was about to open a new avenue of ministry—one that would affect him deeply.

1980 to 2003

Jeff and Karyn in
Egypt, 1998.

Jeff and Karyn
in Israel, 1988.

The family in Israel, 1992.

Jeff and Karyn on the
Mount of Olives, 1993.

Jeffrey and Jeff after being reunited, 1987.

Jeff and Jeffrey, 1991.

The Azusa Pacific graduate with his mom, 1989.

The four brothers: Jeff, Dan, Gary, and Richard.

The family: (top) Richard, Karyn, Kay, Tom (step-dad), Elaine, Gary, (bottom) Jeff, Mom, and Dan.

Chapter

19

It's a Jungle Out There

"I want to recruit you as a volunteer police chaplain."

Tim, a Christian police officer from Montebello, had received the okay to go ahead with a new program. He explained to Jeff that he would be used as a counselor to console crime and accident victims, to help officers cope with the violence they often faced on the streets, and to help with any family problems.

"We would use you for death notifications to families, and if need be, in hostage negotiations," he said to Jeff. He hesitated, then added, "I have to be honest with you. Some of the officers don't really like the idea of having clergy around. But I think once they get to know you, they'll be fine."

Jeff thought back to the time after high school when he briefly considered police work and even took a police science course for a short while. A very short while, considering he was still using drugs.

"How much time would be involved in this?" Jeff asked.

"Right now, we'd like you to sit in on Friday night shift briefings and then ride along with an officer for the night."

Officer Tim and Jeff as a police chaplain, 1981.

Jeff thought about it, prayed about it, and finally agreed to it. He called Tim back, "Yes, I'd like to be a part of something like that. I'd love to be able to share with the guys on the force."

On Friday night, one of the officers came over to Jeff at the briefing and said, "What are you doing here?"

"I'm just here to help however I can," Jeff answered.

"I remember you," he said. "You've got a record."

"Yeah, from when I was young and crazy," Jeff said. He wondered if this was going to be a problem.

"I was involved with the fighting and riots around that time myself," the officer said. His voice was friendly. "Now, look at us. I'm a cop and you're a pastor." He laughed.

On his first ride along, Jeff rode with Tim. A call came in over the radio, giving a location nearby.

"Shots fired! Possible gang shooting."

Tim spun the cruiser around, tires squealing, and sped down a side street, weaving around traffic with the sirens wailing. When they screeched to a halt in front of the house, Jeff realized they were the first ones on the scene. Several people milling around outside pointed to a house and shouted, "In there! Someone's been shot!"

Tim radioed in for an ambulance and for backup. "Come with me," he said to Jeff. He dashed toward the house, gun drawn. "Stay with me, stay close," he ordered. Jeff wondered if someone was inside with a gun waiting to ambush them. He saw a trail of blood as they entered the house.

"Over here," Tim said. A teenager lay bleeding from the chest. Tim checked his wound. "This one got blasted with a shotgun. It doesn't look good." He glanced around and pointed to another teenage boy lying on the floor across the room. "Check him out."

Jeff knelt beside the boy, looking at his blood-soaked shirt. The bullet had struck him in the side. Blood oozed out of the wound and spread to the floor. The boy was still breathing, but he was about to lose consciousness.

"Hang in there," Jeff said to the victim. "Help is on the way."

Tim leaned over him and said, "He's been hit with a .45."

Sirens wailed outside as more police cars converged on the scene. The ambulance arrived and the paramedics came in with stretchers. Jeff stepped aside as they performed with clockwork precision, placing a thick swatch of gauze against the wound, checking his breathing, preparing an IV line, and placing an oxygen mask over the boy's face. Jeff had watched scenes like this in the movies, but it didn't come close to capturing the dehumanizing reality of murder. The homicide unit arrived and investigators talked to those standing around outside, trying to find out what happened. Most weren't talking, other than admitting they had heard gunshots.

"Let's go," Tim finally said. He looked at Jeff and said, "You're a mess."

Jeff looked down at his clothes and hands. They were red with the boy's dried blood. They drove back to the station to clean up.

"Is this the way it is around here? Is this how you spend Friday nights?" Jeff asked. The raw reality of what they had just experienced began to sink in.

"We witness scenes like this more than most people realize," Tim said. "We think it was a gang shooting. Those guys were shot in the alley and dragged into the house."

"Are they going to make it?" Jeff asked.

"One's already dead and the other one is in surgery." He shook his head. "If he makes it, what will he be facing out there in the streets?" His voice reflected the heaviness in his heart.

"Teenage murderers," Jeff thought on his way home that night. He had never dealt with anything so violent. He wondered if the officers ever really became desensitized to it. "It's a jungle out there." He prayed for Tim and the others who were at the scene and for the boys and their families. Hot tears sprang to his eyes as he realized the damage the enemy of our souls can do.

At one point Jeff went to Rio Hondo Police Academy. He made it through and could have gotten a uniform and carried a gun as a reserve officer, but didn't feel that was the direction for him to go. He remained a chaplain volunteer.

Los Angeles Times article, 1988.

On another Friday night ride along, a call came in that there was another shooting, this one a suicide. When Jeff and the officer arrived, a teenage boy was lying dead in a hallway.

"Looks like he blew his brains out with a .45 caliber," the officer said.

Jeff looked around at the scene. Half of the boy's brain was splattered all over, with blood streaks smeared down the wall where he had slid to the floor. The pool of blood beneath the boy soaked the carpet.

The parents sat in their living room in shock, the mother sobbing uncontrollably. "My son, my son," she cried out in despair, clinging to her husband.

"Oh God, help me," Jeff whispered. "What if this were my child?" He managed to find some comforting words to speak to them and stayed by their side while the coroner came and removed the body.

172

"Who cleans this mess up?" Jeff asked one of the officers. The bloody walls and carpet were reminders of the horror.

"Well, we don't," he said. "I guess someone in the family will have to do it."

"What?! After all they've just been through?" Jeff got on his knees and began ripping out the rug in the hallway. Then he found a bucket and cleaning supplies and began scrubbing the blood and flesh from the walls. He gagged and prayed as he scrubbed until his hands were raw. When he finished, he prayed with the parents, offered to assist with funeral arrangements, then left. He cleaned himself up the best he could back at the station, talked with the guys for a while, then started for home.

The bloody scene played itself over and over again in his mind. The twisted body, half of its head missing, the blood. "I can't go home feeling like this," he thought. "Get a grip, Jeff." He drove to the beach, parked the car, walked down to the edge of the water, and sat in the sand. Had anyone ever witnessed to this boy? What was he going through that made him take his own life? It shook him to the depth of his being. He felt the tears rising, sharp and painful, behind his eyes. "Lord, show me how to minister to the deep heartache in this boy's mother and father."

With a heavy sigh, he leaned back and lay down in the sand. He stayed there for a long time, looking up at the stars and listening to the soothing sound of the waves. Comforting Bible passages came to his mind, and he meditated on them. He fully realized now just how stressful law enforcement is, and yet few police officers seek help in coping. When he finally got up to go home, he was more committed than ever to do his best to offer encouragement and comfort to both the victims and the officers. And more importantly, to share Jesus with them.

Shortly after this, he arrived on the scene of a domestic violence situation. He was able to intervene by having the officer take the wife aside while he talked to the husband. Jeff then spoke to them together and convinced them to come to the church for help. During the course of counseling, they accepted the Lord and their lives changed. Scenes like this kept him personally serving as a chaplain volunteer for the next eighteen years.

The newspapers picked up on the story of him serving as a police chaplain, and Jeff was glad to have the opportunity to let people know just how stressful police work is.

"... They see the dark side all the time. It's a thankless job because they very seldom hear good news as far as they are making a dent in what's going on. The pressure that's on them to perform well and perform right is tremendous, because they have to be above reproach, they have to represent the department. There's just a lot of pressure they get from the people in general ... it can be depressing. It's a very depressing environment to be always around.

"The officers I know who are doing really well are the ones who have a spiritual relationship with the Lord. They're able to have a family outside of the police family. They have a church family, and they're balanced. We have a police home Bible study ... Firemen, police officers, paramedics—they have jobs alike and pressures alike—they get together and support each other." [7]

More determined than ever to reach as many people as possible with the hope of the Gospel, to prevent some of these tragedies from occurring, Jeff encouraged more outreach into the community and beyond. The results would be greater than he could have ever imagined.

20

Field Work: Seed and Harvest

Lightworks, one of the new ministries in the church, featured weekly movies, plays, and other entertainment to reach families of the community with the Gospel message. Christian concerts geared toward the youth were held weekly in the main sanctuary. A variety of bands and individual musicians offered their talents, and a pastor would present a message. They also began to bring Christian music out into the community at high schools, convention centers, stadiums, and parks.

Jeff saw the success of the youth concerts his friend, Greg Laurie, did in Costa Mesa. He said to his staff, "We need to do something like that here." He put Mike, one of his pastors, in charge of pulling together an event at Cerritos College stadium. Mike put a committee together, prayer teams, ushers, counselors, set-up and teardown people, and security. The entire pastoral staff came out to help with set-up. Mike looked out at the football field. "What if nobody comes?" he thought. "Maybe we should have played it safe and started on a smaller scale." Just then, Jeff walked up to him.

"The Lord is going to do something exciting here!" he said to Mike.

The night of the concert, Mike met with the prayer team up in the press box. He paced back and forth as he prayed.

"Look!" someone said, pointing out to the field. It was early, but the chairs in the field were already full. The bleachers were filling up fast and cars were still coming.

"Praise God!" Mike shouted. "Hallelujah!"

When the concert was over and they reviewed the numbers of those who came forward to accept the Lord, Mike was amazed. He realized what a tremendous vision God had laid on Jeff's heart. He whispered a prayer of thanks for the privilege of serving with him.

Another time they held a concert at the Anaheim Convention Center with the popular and radical Christian rock 'n' roll band, Stryper. They were controversial with traditional church folk because of their makeup and body suits.

"We have to be willing to take risks," Jeff said. "The Lord will use them to bring in the youth of the community." The crowds came, and again, many accepted the Lord.

"So many are coming to us out of drug and alcohol addiction," Jeff said to the staff one day, "we need to pray for someone to lead a ministry for them."

That's when Steve and Linda Everett came to the church. They had come out of addiction themselves just three years before, and when Jeff heard their story, he asked them to come to his office.

"We've been praying to start a support group for those coming out of addiction," Jeff said. "The only group I know of is over at Calvary Chapel Bellflower with John Rutherford. Would you be willing to go over there and see what he's doing, spend some time with him?"

Steve agreed to check it out and ended up sitting under John's mentoring for a full year. Jeff called him into his office again.

"Do you think it's time to start this type of ministry here?" he asked Steve.

"Well, you have one or two people on staff who could handle it," Steve answered. He really didn't feel like starting something himself. He was enjoying being with John's group.

"The pastors are really busy," Jeff said. "They don't have time to take this on."

Steve and Linda sat there in silence for a few moments.

"Well, I suppose if no one else is going to do it, I'll do it," Steve said.

"That's what I wanted to hear!" Jeff said. Then he became serious. "Count the cost," he said. "This means a solid commitment to be here every Tuesday night to lead a group."

Steve agreed and when they got outside he turned to Linda and said, "Why didn't you say anything in there? I don't really feel qualified to do this."

"Steve, God is going to move with or without you. He's doing something, and we're going to be part of it."

When he first started, Steve ran the ministry like other nationally known self-help groups. Then the Lord showed him that what the addicted in his group needed was the 'one-step' approach. After they accepted Jesus into their lives, they needed more than just deliverance from substance abuse—they needed to get right with the Lord and be healed completely. They needed to learn how to walk in their sobriety, walk in their deliverance, and walk in their healing. Because all sin is addictive, they needed to get into the Bible and learn how to apply truths of the Word of God to every situation in their lives. So, Steve began to operate in his gift of teaching.

At first, when he made this change, the group got smaller because those involved were used to another format. Steve remembered hearing Alan Redpath at a conference say, "Sometimes you have to empty a church before you can fill it." He clung to that idea and soon the group exploded with people.

One girl came who had anorexia and bulimia. Steve prayed for her after the teaching, and she came back the following week with a big smile on her face.

"This is the first week in five years that I ate food and didn't throw it up," she said. She had applied the teaching to her situation. Steve determined not to ever put God in a box again, but to remain open to however God wanted to lead.

He had to divide the ministry into many smaller support groups and develop leaders over them—each leader had come out of some form of addiction themselves. They named the support groups "New Hope Ministries," and expanded to include problems with drugs, alcohol, codependency, spousal abuse, adult children of alcoholics, overeaters, anorexia, and other special groups for men, women, and teenagers, regardless of whether their problem was fear or some other form of addiction. They became known as the Intensive Care Unit (ICU) of the church.

Jeff started a radio program called "Sound Doctrine." It began broadcasting Monday through Friday in Southern California, Chicago, and Philadelphia, with a combined potential listening audience in the millions. With the responses coming in, it was obvious that people's lives were being touched and changed. Jeff can now be heard on CSN throughout the nation and KWVE, 107.9 FM in Southern California. It's exciting to see God's Word come alive—it's true, "faith comes by *hearing* and that of the Word of God!"

One Sunday morning after a service, Jeff stood outside the sanctuary greeting everyone as usual. A tough looking Mexican man came up to him.

"I'm Mark Maciel," he said. His broad and muscular features combined with his Fu Manchu beard gave him an intimidating appearance. "I accepted the Lord while in prison, and I'm looking for a home church."

"Let's get together and talk," Jeff replied.

178

They met that week and Mark shared with Jeff the story of how he came out of a life of crime and drugs and how Jesus turned his life around.

"What do you feel called to do with your life?"

"I'm already involved in some volunteer jail ministry," Mark said. "I think that's what God wants me to do. He's given me many opportunities to share my testimony."

"Great. I want you to meet with one of the men from the church who has started a small outreach to the local juvenile hall. Give him your input, then get back to me and keep me informed."

Mark ended up being asked to run the New Life Prison Ministry, married a member of the church, Patricia, and eventually came on staff full-time. He oversaw the chaplains' program for the Los Angeles County Sheriff's Department, and he started a men's home called House of Jeremiah and a women's home called House of Esther. The ministry helped those coming out of prison by providing a place to live, assisting them with finding a job, getting them grounded in their faith, and generally helping them to settle into their new life.

"I'd like you to come speak to the men at the prison," Mark said to Jeff one day. "They listen to you on the radio, and it would be a big deal to them if you would come and speak."

He agreed and many came forward for prayer when Jeff finished. Another time Mark was doing an outreach at Cook County Jail in Chicago at the same time that Neil Matranga was planning an outreach in Chicago in connection with the radio program. Once again, Mark invited Jeff to speak. As a guard escorted them into the jail, the chill of the concrete walls and the clang of the steel gates closing tightly behind them made Jeff shudder.

"This is very intimidating," he said.

"Prison is like this," Mark said.

After that, Jeff said to Mark, "This ministry is important. Whatever God is putting on your heart, you go for it."

A few people in the church established a Committee of Helps to show the love of God in practical ways to the community. They maintained a food bank, a stock of clothes, blankets, and furniture to distribute to those in poverty or those affected by disaster. They provided meals and transportation to those who needed them, provided baby-sitting in emergencies, and sometimes provided plumbing, carpentry, or electrical services when special needs arose. A real spirit of cooperation and love brought the people of the church together to serve their community.

Another group of thirty people in the church formed the Convalescent Ministry, visiting the sick and the elderly. This naturally led to establishing a hospice program, providing supportive care for terminally ill patients and their families. A team of workers made themselves available twenty-four hours a day, seven days a week.

Jeff's vision of reaching out to people grew beyond the local community. He put together many missions trips, sometimes with other pastors, but always including some of the leadership and members of the church. They traveled to many foreign countries. They continued to go to Mexico on a regular basis, then, as opportunities came up, traveled to the Middle East, Africa, Russia, and Egypt. He brought financial support for churches in Beirut, Lebanon, and assisted in the feeding camps of Ethiopia sponsored by World Vision.

Jeff and Karyn's daughter, Christy, a teenager at the time, went with him to the feeding camps. Although World Vision had supplied an abundance of food, so many starving children came to the camp that the food began to run out.

"We have to decide which children to give the remaining food to," one of the leaders said. He choked up. "The rest will have to be turned away."

"Does that mean the others will die?" Christy asked, horrified. She clutched a little baby in her arms.

He didn't answer. Christy burst into tears, and Jeff and the other volunteers all began to weep.

Jeff returned home more determined than ever to reach as many people as he could, knowing that many would receive a call on their lives to serve in the mission fields of the world. He thought about Matthew 9:37, "The harvest truly is plenteous, but the labourers are few."

On another trip to Beirut, Lebanon, right after the bombing of the Marine Base where 263 died, with fighting and bombing all around, Jeff had two Lebanese men drive him into a certain area to find a general who had given Jeff permission to come talk to his men.

They drove past bombed-out villages, and then the jeep stopped at a roadblock. Two soldiers scrambled out from behind a wall of sandbags and ran down the dirt road toward the vehicle, aiming their guns, ready to fire. Jeff

Jeff with two Marines, Beirut, Lebanon, 1983.

hit the floor in the backseat and the two Lebanese men crouched, trembling in the front seat. After much shouting, everyone was ordered out of the vehicle.

"You're an American!" one of the soldiers said to Jeff.

"Yes, I'm Pastor Jeff Johnson. I'm here to speak to the men and teach a Bible study." He tried to remain calm.

Jeff in a Beirut bunker with U.S. soldiers, 1983.

"You're lucky we didn't blow you away," he said. "Yesterday we had a skirmish here and we had to blow up a jeep on this very spot. Everyone in it was killed."

It was then that Jeff remembered. At that exact time, a group in the church in California was having a prayer meeting for him. "Thank You, Lord," he whispered.

Another time Jeff went to Peru because one of the church staff was Peruvian and still had family there.

"Let's do a concert over there," Jeff said. "They produce great results here, why not there?"

A few involved in the planning of the outreach weren't sure. Peru was different. But they forged ahead and planned a concert and a skateboard demonstration to attract the youth. Jeff's friend, Pastor Raul Ries, agreed to participate and shared his testimony of coming from violence and fury to freedom in Christ. Tara, Jeff's daughter, then fifteen years old, was one of the singers. Over fifteen thousand attended and thousands came forward to accept the Lord. This was the national stadium's first concert and the largest event ever held there. One of the young men who came forward that night later became the pastor of Calvary Chapel of Lima, Peru.

When Russia opened up, Jeff went there on a two-week mission trip with Jeff Fadness and several other staff members. They got permission from the assistant mayor of Vladimir to hold Christian concerts and discovered that every factory had a theater, formerly used for communist indoctrination. They went to the head of several of the factories, getting permission to come in and use the theaters. A small church was started in a hotel to help the new believers grow in their faith. Jeff and Christina Fadness pastored the church, Calvary Chapel of Vladimir. Al and Susie Harb, with their kids, and Ron Castro joined with them to head up the missions teams that began going to Russia on a regular basis. Four additional Calvary Chapels began in Russia, all of which were led by national pastors.

Tim Lamb felt called to North Africa to begin church planting among the Muslims. This had to be done in secret because open Christian churches are not allowed. With assistance from the U.S. government, he began working with an agency to feed over fourteen thousand malnourished mothers and children every month. He learned the Arabic dialects and lived among the poor, in one room, with no running water.

Tom Maxwell began leading missions teams into the Philippines and later felt called to move there to minister in Cebu.

From the outreach in Mexico, the church took over an orphanage that was about to close. Tomas and Maricela Shockey responded to the call to become the directors of the orphanage. Tony, one of the

Jeff today, as he continues to surf.

young boys Jeff met there on one of their first missions trips to Mexico, later became a pastor. Every summer, Calvary Chapel of Downey sends out many short-term missionary teams, and the church continues to support many full-time missionaries.

Jeff often took his surfboard along on missions trips, pulling away from the groups briefly to enjoy the surfing in Israel, Peru, and Mexico. He especially enjoyed a few outreach trips to Hawaii. Their annual trips to Israel were a highlight for Jeff and Karyn. They always encouraged those who had never been there to consider going with them.

Jeff and David Kidron, our tour guide to Israel for the past 30 years.

"Everyone needs to go at least once," Jeff said to a staff member. "It's eye-opening. You understand the Bible stories in a different way when you see the land and how close everything is. The Bible comes alive to you." This annual Israel trip continues, with David Kidron as its faithful tour guide.

What Jeff didn't know was that his next trip to Israel would change their life and Karyn's ministry direction. And it would eventually open the door for her to share the secret she had held inside for so many years.

Chapter

21

The Secret Revealed

Jeff and Karyn stood in awe gazing at the beautiful architecture of St. Ann's Cathedral in Jerusalem, which is located near the Pool of Bethesda. Others gathered around to hear the tour guide give a brief talk. Afterwards, Karyn noticed one of the women quietly weeping.

"Can I help?" Karyn asked, gently putting her arm around the woman.

"I'm sorry," she said, "It's just that this reminds me of my young niece who happens to be in St. Ann's Maternity Home in Los Angeles." She dabbed at her eyes with a tissue. "She's having a baby and wants to give it up for adoption."

"Is that a problem for the family?"

"It's just that we'll never know how the baby turns out or what kind of a home she'll be placed in."

Without thinking it through, Karyn offered, "I know a couple in our church who is looking to adopt a baby. Maybe we could get them together."

When they returned to the States, Karyn contacted everyone and assisted with the arrangements, which ultimately led to the baby's adoption. Karyn's eyes blurred with tears as the baby was dedicated in the church. She felt so good to know that this child would be brought up in a loving, Christian home.

After the service, a pregnant teenager came up to her and asked, "Do you think you could find me a family like that?" Her eyes pleaded with Karyn. "I know I'm not ready to be a mother, but I want my baby to be brought up in a good home."

Over the next six months, Karyn assisted in placing six babies with Christian adoptive parents. "I've run out of friends who want to adopt," Karyn said jokingly to Jeff one day. "What do I do when the next request comes in?"

"God seems to be doing something here," he said. "You need to pray about it." He looked lovingly at his wife, realizing how much his love had grown towards her. He was thankful that she had overcome her agoraphobia and was fully dedicated to serving the Lord. He put his arms around her and said, "Christy and Tara are such a blessing in our lives, and I'm sure there are other couples out there who would love to have children."

The whole concept of open adoption blossomed and developed in Karyn's mind and heart. She loved working with the girls. The ministry formalized into the House of Ruth, and within two years, they were assisting in one hundred adoptions per year, one of the largest Christian adoption services in the state of California. Karyn hired two women to work on staff with her because it became more than she could handle alone.

"I feel so unqualified to do this," Karyn said to her mother one day. "I've only got a year's worth of nurses' training."

"Why don't you go back to school and get your degree in social welfare?" her mother suggested.

"I'm so busy now," Karyn moaned, "how could I possibly attend school?"

"Don't make such a big deal of it," she said. "Just take three units at a time. You can do it."

She took her mother's advice and started taking the necessary classes. Her mother died during this period, and

Karyn felt the loss deeply. Plus, it reminded her of the secret she had kept from Jeff. Her mother had advised her never to tell him. But Karyn knew that wasn't right. She, Jeff, and the girls were getting ready for a short surfing trip to Mexico. She decided to tell him there.

One night, in the vacation trailer, while Jeff was watching Billy Graham on TV, Karyn got down on her knees in the bedroom.

"Lord, I've messed up so many things in my life. And this secret has been the deepest pain in my heart." Tears glistened on her face. "I can't do this on my own, I need Your help. It's going to change our lives forever." She thought of the Bible story about Jesus and the ninety-nine sheep and felt impressed that she was supposed to read it, but couldn't remember where it was. She dried her tears and went to Jeff.

"Do you know where that story is about Jesus and the sheep?" she asked.

"Matthew 18 and again in Luke 15," he said.

She went back to the bedroom and opened her Bible. She wept as she read how Jesus left the ninety-nine and went searching for the one that was lost, and how the neighbors rejoiced when it was found. "If people are going to rejoice with me, they have to know."

She ran back to Jeff and said, "I've got something to tell you."

"Just a minute," he said, holding up his hand. "I want to hear this song."

Karyn sat down next to him and listened as George Beverly Shea's rich voice sang, "There were ninety and nine that safely lay in the shelter of the fold. But one was out on the hills away ..." Tears blinded her eyes and slid down her face as the words of the song penetrated her heart.

"What's going on?" Jeff asked.

"I need to tell you something." She swallowed hard and held her tears in check.

"Is this the thing you've been trying to tell me for years?" He braced himself.

"Yes, it is." She took a deep breath. "I'm going to tell you now." She was silent for a moment.

"Yeah, right," he said.

"No really, I'm going to tell you." She blurted out, "I had a baby before we were married."

"Well, I know that," he said.

"No, no, not Christy. I had another baby. And I gave her up for adoption."

"A baby?" He let out a long sigh. "That's it? That's the big secret after all these years?"

"Will you forgive me?" Karyn asked.

"Forgive you?" He laughed. "Man, I thought you were a homosexual or something. Or that maybe you murdered someone and buried him in cement somewhere!"

"You'd forgive me for murder?" Karyn looked shocked.

"I love you," he said. "Forgiving you is not a problem." He shook his head. "A baby. This has all been about a baby?" He looked at her and said, "I've done that myself. Remember my teenage years? My girlfriend Debbie had a baby."

"Yeah, but you hated Debbie for giving yours away."

"I didn't believe it was mine," Jeff reminded her. "I still don't think it was."

They talked a long time, and Karyn told him what had happened to her. She was a sophomore in high school when she got pregnant, and her mother gave her no choice about what to do. She was secretly sent off to a home for unwed mothers where her baby was taken from her and given up for adoption. Her mother told family and friends that Karyn was attending a Catholic boarding school for a year. She had to live the lie.

"I had a beautiful, blue-eyed baby girl," she said. "I feel like the mother of Moses who had to place her baby in a basket in the river, not knowing where he would end up." The tears surfaced again. Jeff put his arms around her.

"I can't believe this has been such a deep problem for you," he said. "Giving the baby up wasn't even your choice."

"I need to find her," Karyn said. "I recently talked to a search consultant, and he told me that if I pay them a fee, I'll have her name and current address in my hand, although legally I can't contact her until she's eighteen years old unless her parents give their permission. I just want to know that she's okay. I don't want to complicate her life or cause pain for her adoptive parents."

"It's okay. Do what you need to do."

"Do you remember the time you asked me why I made a birthday cake? It was for her. Natalie. That's what I named her. Her adoptive parents named her Linda. I celebrated her birthday every year by myself."

"I wish I had known," Jeff said.

"There's something else," she said. "I know that Debbie's baby was yours. She was my friend at that time and I know. She had a boy."

"I have a son?" He leaned back on the sofa, trying to absorb all this.

The next morning Karyn took Christy for a walk down to the beach. She left Tara with Jeff, feeling that maybe she was a little young to understand. She would tell her later.

"Christy, there's something I have to tell you."

"What is it?" she asked. "You look so serious."

Karyn sat down and started writing in the sand. Christy watched. First, she wrote Christy, then Tara, and above Christy's name, Natalie.

"Who's Natalie?"

"She's your sister."

"I have a sister?" She was quiet for a moment, and then said, "Mom, somehow I always knew there was something, a secret. I just didn't know what it was."

Back at home after their vacation, Karyn used her connections in the adoption field to begin an inquiry to find their missing children. One day when she came home from the House of Ruth, Tara was sitting in the living room crying.

"What's wrong?" Karyn asked.

"Dad and I were watching *Little House on the Prairie* and Dad

Tara, Karyn, Linda, and Christy, 1986.

said to me, 'You know how Albert is adopted on this show?' I said, 'Yeah, I knew Albert was adopted.' Then he said to me, 'You have a brother who was given up for adoption.'" Her tears choked her words. "He didn't know what else to say. I think he was trying not to get emotional, so he just walked out of the room."

Karyn gathered her up in her arms and sighed. "Well, Tara, it's true. You do have a brother." She hesitated, and then added, "And I might as well tell you now that you also have another sister."

"What?!"

Christy stepped into the room and asked, "What's going on here?"

"I told Tara about your sister, Linda."

"Oh, I already knew about that, Tara," Christy said.

"Do you know about Jeffrey too?" Tara asked.

"Jeffrey? Who's Jeffrey?"

"We have a brother!"

Christy looked at Karyn. "Is there more I don't know about?" She started crying too. "I don't believe this."

Jeff came back and everyone was crying. They finally calmed down and had a long talk, sharing with the girls what had happened.

"I already know that Linda is in a Christian home, with a stay-at-home mom, and she has a brother four years older than her," Karyn said. "Just like me and your Uncle Rusty."

"And I didn't think the baby that Debbie had was mine," Jeff said. "She had another boyfriend around the same time."

"She named him Jeffrey," Karyn said, looking at Jeff. "I found that out too." She hadn't had a chance to tell him yet.

"Jeffrey," Jeff said. "Wow."

"Can we meet them?" Christy asked.

"Because of the way they were adopted, we legally can't do that until they are eighteen years old. But we can be praying for them."

When Linda was seventeen, Karyn felt a strong impression inside that it was time to contact her. "I need Your help, Lord." She talked with Jeff first.

"Before I meet Linda and all this family stuff becomes public, we need to tell the church," Karyn said. "We can't keep it a secret anymore."

Jeff agreed and they decided to share the whole story with the married couples' Christmas gathering at the church. From there, they were sure the word would spread. Jeff also shared it individually with pastoral staff members, giving them permission to tell others.

"I need to tell my brother, Rusty, and Robyn first," Karyn said. "That's going to be hard. I don't know if he'll understand why I kept this in the dark for so long, the guilt and shame that I felt, the pressure from my mother to keep it a secret."

"That was a different era," Jeff said. "It was a generation that didn't talk about those things."

"But it was like it never happened," Karyn said. "I even said to my mother, 'We're Baptist. Who in the world is going to believe that you sent me away to a Catholic boarding school?' My dad went along with the decision. I can't believe that people bought the story. She drilled it into my head over and over that I was not to discuss this with anyone."

After they told everyone, Karyn contacted the agency that had handled Linda's adoption.

"I want to contact Linda," she said.

"No. Not until she's eighteen," the social worker said. "And even then, it's up to her, *if* she wants to see you." Her voice was cold and exact.

"Look," Karyn said, "I've known for some time where Linda is, and I haven't contacted her. I haven't caused any problems. But now I want to see my daughter. I'm simply asking you to contact the mother and see if she's open to it. Tell her who I am and give her my phone number."

"Fine," she said. "We'll contact her."

The social worker called back days later to say that the family wanted to wait until Linda was eighteen and had graduated from high school. Disappointed, Karyn kept praying that God would open the door. About a month later, she answered a call at her ministry office.

"My name is Carolyn," she said. "Do you work with Pastor Jeff Johnson?"

"Yes, I do," Karyn said. "May I help you?"

"Do you know him pretty well?"

"Yes, I know him really well."

"Well, I listen to him every day on the radio, his 'Sound Doctrine' program."

"I'm his wife, Karyn."

Carolyn choked up. "I'm Linda's mother," she said.

Surprised, Karyn had to catch her breath. "I thought you didn't want contact with me."

"Once the agency told me who you were, and I knew about your family because of the radio program, well, I changed my mind." Her voice grew serious. "Is Pastor Jeff the father?"

"No," Karyn said. "I was very young and had no relationship with Jeff at that time."

They talked for a while and an instant bond developed between them. They made a plan for Karyn to come to their house to meet Linda.

Karyn arrived at the house with a bouquet of flowers and a homemade Raggedy Ann doll with a red heart that said Natalie, the name she had given Linda at birth. Trembling, Karyn knocked on the door and smoothed out her red top and tan pants.

Linda came to the door wearing a red top and tan pants. They stared at each other for a moment, and then laughed nervously. Karyn felt like she was looking into a mirror, they were so much alike. They hugged awkwardly. The visit went well. They looked through photo albums of Linda growing up, and discovered just how many mannerisms, likes, and dislikes she and Linda had in common.

"I always had this faceless woman in my mind who was my birth mother," Linda said, "and I felt like I had two sisters somewhere."

"You do," Karyn said. "Christy and Tara."

Karyn took her out for lunch and said, "I have another gift for you." She removed a small jewelry box from her purse. "I bought this on your sixteenth birthday."

Karyn gave her a gold ring with a teardrop shaped gem, her birthstone. "This is for all the tears I cried for you," she said. "I've celebrated all your birthdays." Her eyes misted.

After lunch they drove around town and Linda showed Karyn her high school and the Baptist church she attended. They chatted the whole time. Karyn didn't like some of what Linda told her, but she appreciated her honesty.

Later at home, Karyn told Jeff, "I can't believe how much she's like me. She even walks like me. And she likes ice cubes in her milk. Can you believe it?" She sighed. "The problem is, she's repeating all the same mistakes I made. She openly told me she's using drugs and dating a lot of boys." Tears cornered her eyes. "She got pregnant at age fifteen, but had a miscarriage and lost the baby."

"God brought her into our lives at this time for a reason," Jeff said. "Maybe with God's help, we can point her in the right direction."

They spent quality time with Linda, welcoming her into their home, but Karyn challenged her on her lifestyle. They had laid out some strict rules with Christy and Tara about dating; they were clear about what was permissible and what wasn't. Now they had Linda bringing in non-Christian guys, along with attitudes and activities that weren't acceptable.

When Linda graduated from high school, she got heavily into the party scene, and her adoptive parents finally asked her to leave the house if she was going to continue. She rebelled even further by moving into an apartment with her boyfriend. Karyn talked with her one day about her drug use.

"You've got to stop doing drugs," she said. "It's going to destroy you."

"Why should I stop?" Linda asked defiantly. "I like drugs."

"You know what?" Karyn said, "Why don't you just tell the Lord that you don't want to stop." Her eyes caught and held her daughter's. "See what He has to say about it."

"Fine," Linda said.

"Tell Him you like it and you don't want to stop. And if He wants you to stop, ask Him to do something about it."

(clockwise) Jeffrey Linda, Christy, and Tara, 1990.

That night Linda got loaded, then remembered what Karyn had told her. She looked up at the sky and said, "Lord, I like this feeling. And I'm probably going to do it again tomorrow. So if You want me to stop, You're going to have to do something because I like doing it."

She had an extreme allergic reaction to the drugs and her throat swelled up, frightening her. But later, after the crisis, she thought it had been a coincidence—bad drugs. The next time she used, the same thing happened. She

195

finally quit smoking pot and using cocaine, but continued drinking alcohol.

Sometimes she stayed with Jeff and Karyn, but it became obvious that Linda was a very independent spirit, and they were concerned about the influence she may have on Christy and Tara. Up to that point, Christy and Tara were handling their teen years very well. They were involved in church, youth group, and the purity seminars that Karyn spoke at in many different churches, challenging teens to keep themselves sexually pure until marriage.

"It's like there's a bad spirit in our home," Jeff said to Karyn one day. "I don't mean that Linda is the bad spirit; it's the friends and activities she brings into the house. It's beginning to affect all of us. We can't allow this to invade our home and affect the whole family."

"I don't want her to think we don't love her," Karyn said.

"I know it's hard," Jeff said, "but we can't lower our standards for her. We have to have the same rules for her as we do for Christy and Tara. Some tough love is needed here."

Karyn reluctantly agreed and had a talk with Linda. Jeff and Karyn challenged her to get her life right before God. Linda responded by saying that she would marry the guy she was living with.

"That's not what we had in mind," Jeff said. "We don't think this is a good relationship for you."

But Linda said she was going to marry him with or without their approval. So Jeff performed the ceremony after some premarital counseling at her church in Saugus. The marriage was in crisis from the beginning.

Now it was Jeff's turn to meet his son, Jeffrey.

Karyn had already begun the search process. She paid a fee, and the investigation began with the maternity home where he was born. They discovered his full name was Jeffrey Rosen, and he lived in Huntington Beach.

"It's hard for me to fathom that I've had a son all these years," Jeff said. "I've missed so much." He sighed and looked at Karyn. "So how do we contact him?"

"How about the phone book?" Karyn smiled.

The first phone call turned out to be the right one.

"Does Jeffrey Rosen live here?" Jeff asked.

"Yes, but he's not here right now."

The family wanted Jeff to wait until Jeffrey was eighteen, which was only months away. Then Jeffrey could decide for himself what he wanted to do. They agreed.

When the day arrived, Jeffrey and his parents said they would meet at a local restaurant. Out in the parking lot, everyone stared as Jeff and Jeffrey greeted each other. There was no question that they were birth father and son. Seeing was believing. They looked, walked, and sounded the same. Jeff felt like he was looking at a younger version of himself. They hugged and went inside. The conversation was a little awkward for everyone at first, and they pretty much stuck to small talk. Their family was Jewish.

A short time later, Jeffrey came to the house to meet Christy and Tara, and he was very friendly and open. He told them how, when he was young, he found his birth certificate in a closet with the parental information all blacked out. He always wondered who he really was. Jeff listened to him and was in awe again at how alike they were. At one point, Jeff contacted Jeffrey's birth mother, Debbie, in Oregon to let her know he had found Jeffrey.

"You've got to come down here," Jeff said. "I found our son. You've got to see him."

197

She came down and the three of them met together at a restaurant. Debbie cried when she saw her son. Jeff told Jeffrey that he was sorry for what had happened, and he hoped they could begin to form a relationship. They did, and Jeffrey even went on a couple of trips to Israel with them. Karyn teased them about their mannerisms and how they even talked alike. It was like seeing Jeff in his early years with his hippie lifestyle. They both really loved Jeffrey and were grateful to God for bringing him into the family.

In fact, they had much to be grateful for, not only in their family, but also for the church. Several Calvary Chapels had already started as an outgrowth of their ministry. What they didn't fully realize at the time was that they were entering yet another wave of growth which would require some serious decisions.

Chapter

22

Enlarge the Place of Your Tent

Once again, the church was bursting at the seams with three full Sunday morning services, seating fifteen hundred in each service. This didn't include the Sunday school attendance held simultaneously in the classrooms above the sanctuary. The church board held a meeting to discuss what to do next.

"I've done some figuring," the administrator Neil Matranga said, and it will take about three million dollars to complete the building."

"We could ask for pledges," someone suggested.

"I don't want to pump the people for money," Jeff said. "I know we could take an offering on Wednesday nights and at all the other meetings, but I don't think we should do that."

After discussing various options, Jeff said, "Let's first be sure the people are behind us on this expansion. Let's hold a service in the empty facility and ask the people if they really want to do this. We're going to take a one-time special offering. If we come up with $100,000 to put down towards a loan, we'll move forward."

"One hundred thousand dollars in one offering?"

"Yes," Jeff said. "Then we'll know God is in it—it's His timing, and the people will see that."

They received the money, and borrowed the rest, with a goal of paying it off in fifteen years. As they completed the remainder of the building, their ministry expanded to include a two-year Bible college, and the Christian school expanded to include high school. This meant building a gym for their sports programs, which included football, wrestling, basketball, and volleyball. They built a weight room, an outside playground for the younger kids, a combination cafeteria / mini-chapel, a multi-purpose room with a stage, a library, a computer lab, biology and chemistry labs, art and music rooms, and more. The original south sanctuary offered the opportunity to hold Spanish services on Sundays, and later, Arabic services as well. The new sanctuary seated thirty-five hundred at each service, and attendance continued to increase. Once again, the newspapers picked up on the expansion and a reporter interviewed Neil Matranga, the church administrator.

> *"Calvary Chapel of Downey has 'no membership, no mailing list, nothing on paper,' says church administrator Neil Matranga. 'We do a periodic "loose" head count to get a feel for how many are there (attending services).'*
>
> *"The church has also converted a former gas service station at the south edge of the parcel into a book store and the House of Ruth, an 'adoption ministry' in which mothers-to-be with unwanted pregnancies have a say in placing their babies."* [8]

Pastor Chuck Smith came from Costa Mesa to speak at the dedication service for the new sanctuary. Jeff made a few comments, and then introduced him.

"The Bible says that God's Word will not return void. It goes out and accomplishes its purpose. It's awesome. My pastor, Chuck Smith, taught me that. It grabbed hold of my life, and I'm amazed at what God has done. Pastor Chuck, it's so good to have you, my spiritual father, to be a part of this dedication. Would you come and minister God's Word to us?"

"It's hard for me to describe the joy and the thrill that I have being with you here tonight," he said. "We've watched Calvary Downey from its birth, and what a joy it is to see the way the Lord has blessed and prospered. God has done such a fabulous work." He looked over at Jeff. "What a joy to live long enough to see the fruit of what God has done! This is a special occasion." He turned to the audience and continued.

"I'm reminded of Psalm 73, which begins, 'Truly God is good.' Now that's a basic foundational truth. It's important that you have certain basic truths to rest on. As a child of God, you're going to face a lot of things that you don't know and you don't understand and things that will challenge what you do know. God is good, but there are times when the circumstances of my life would challenge that truth.

"Satan says, 'if God is good, then why did He allow this bad thing to happen to you?' He challenges these basic foundational truths. When I come up with something I don't know, I always fall back on something I DO know. And I know God is good. Never give up what you do know for what you don't know.

"Satan will try to divert your attention away from God and get your eyes on the world around you. As soon as he has your ear, he uses half-truths, and then lies. 'Look at the wicked people who seem prosperous,' he'll whisper. In other words, it doesn't pay to serve God and live right. But read on. It says in verse 17 that when he went into the sanctuary of God, then he understood their end. He got an entirely new perspective on life.

"Sometimes we lose the eternal perspective. As we dedicate this facility to the Lord, it is our prayer that this will be a sanctuary of God where those people who have been beaten and battered by the world, as they come in, will come into the consciousness of the eternal, loving, good God. They will get a new perspective that will be life-transforming." Chuck bowed his head to pray.

"Father, we thank You for the hours, the days, and the years that have gone into the developing of this place—from a store dispensing material things to a house of God imparting eternal life to men and women. Now that it is complete, functional, and operational, we desire to give it back to You. Lord, it's not ours. It's Yours. This is Your sanctuary where people may come and find refuge, find strength, find comfort, and be ministered to by Your Spirit and be healed through Your Word. We dedicate it to Your honor and glory."

Jeff closed the service. "Paul, in Ephesians, says that Jesus is the chief cornerstone. The Lord wants this house and your house to be built on the solid rock that will stand when the storms come. If you haven't dedicated your life to the Lord, come and do that tonight."

Jeff's prayer proved to be prophetic because at that time, there were new, unrealized storms brewing—in his own home.

Chapter

23

Prodigal Daughters

Returning from a trip to Israel, Karyn and Jeff talked about how well things were going at the church.

"Every time we go to Israel now, I think of the House of Ruth and how it really got started on one of these trips." Karyn reflected for a moment, then added, "And it makes me think of finding Linda. It's strange how at first I never put together in my mind the calling to work with pregnant girls, and how it really came out of my own personal experience with having Linda."

"I hope she's doing okay," Jeff said. "I just don't know if their marriage will survive. At least she's trying to make it work."

"So many parents go through rough years with their teenagers, but we've really been blessed with Christy and Tara," Karyn said. "They sure haven't given us any major problems. It's so great having them come with me to the purity seminars."

"Yes, we're definitely blessed," he said. "Tara's singing has really developed, and I'm glad she's using it for the Lord."

They pulled into their driveway and Karyn went inside the house while Jeff got their suitcases. Christy greeted her mother at the door.

"Welcome home," she said, giving her a quick hug. "How was the trip?"

"It was great," Karyn said, "like every other one we've taken to Israel." She tossed her purse on the sofa and sat down. She looked at Christy. "You look different somehow."

"You just haven't seen me in awhile," she said. Her voice had a nervous pitch to it.

"Hi Mom." Tara came into the room and sat beside Karyn. "Are you hungry?"

"A little," Karyn said. "But what I really want is a nice hot shower."

"Christy and I are going to fix lunch," Tara said. "Enjoy your shower."

When Karyn stepped out of the shower, she realized she hadn't unpacked yet, so she didn't have her hairbrush. She got dressed, then went to Christy's room and reached into her purse for her brush. When she pulled it out, a piece of paper fell out onto the floor. She picked it up to put it back, but suddenly realized what she was looking at. She froze.

"Jeff!" she called. He was in the shower and didn't hear her. She went to the kitchen. "What's this?" she demanded of Christy, placing the paper on the table. "Is it what I think it is?"

"Oh, no," Christy gasped. "Mom, I was going to tell you." She burst into tears.

"Is it yours?!"

"Is what yours?" Jeff asked, stepping into the room.

"This sonogram!" Karyn said, picking it up and waving it in front of Christy. "Apparently, she's pregnant."

Christy hung her head. Jeff stood there staring at the sonogram. Karyn lost control.

"How could you do this?" she shouted. "How could you come and speak with me at the purity seminars, then turn right around and do this?!" Her voice rose. "Didn't that purity promise mean anything to you? Was it all just a phony front?"

"Mom, I'm sorry," Christy cried. "Look, I'll just leave. I'll leave the church quietly so I won't embarrass you and Dad." She ran out of the kitchen into the bathroom and slammed the door. Sobs racked her body.

Tara just stood there, not saying anything. Karyn looked over at her.

"I just found out two days ago," Tara said. "We were going to tell you in a few days, right after Thanksgiving."

"I just can't believe this," Karyn said, tears streaming down her face now.

"Karyn," Jeff said, "this isn't helping. We need to calm down and talk this out. We don't even know who the father is."

"The father!" She hadn't even thought of that yet. She marched to the bathroom door and yelled, "Who's the father, Christy?!"

"Okay, okay," Jeff said. "No more of this." He put his arm around Karyn. "Come on. Let's sit down." Then he called to Christy. "Come on out, Christy, let's talk."

They all sat in the living room.

"Dad, just let me leave. I'll just leave."

"No," he said, "I don't want you to leave."

"But the church ..." she started crying again. "I'm so ashamed."

"Don't you worry about the church," he said. "That's my responsibility."

"So who's the father?" Karyn asked more calmly this time.

"Kenny," she murmured. (Kenny was a childhood friend from school.)

"We thought that was over," Jeff said.

"I've been seeing him secretly."

Karyn put her head in her hands.

"We'll just get married," Christy said.

"No!" Karyn forced herself to settle down. "I don't think he's right for you. I'm concerned about his relationship with the Lord. You just don't rush into something that serious."

"Your mother is right," Jeff said. "His walk with the Lord doesn't appear to be a priority to him. At some point, that will be a problem to you if it doesn't change. You know that. Marriage is much too serious a commitment to take lightly."

A few months later, Christy went into labor. Jeff and Karyn were by her side in the hospital, with Jeff taking pictures. In spite of the difficult circumstances, this was their grandchild. When Christy groaned in pain, Jeff held her hand and said, "It's okay, honey. Just ride the labor pains like a wave. Like you're surfing."

"Dad!" She glared at him. "You have no idea what this feels like!"

Karyn glanced at Jeff. "She's right. Don't push it."

Laura was born. She and Christy went home to live with Jeff and Karyn. They made it clear that they didn't want Christy to date Kenny. Christy obeyed for a while, but she still had feelings for him.

In the middle of Christy's crisis, Tara met someone—a Marine. Tara was leading one of the discussion groups for the youth Bible study at church. A good-looking Latino boy attended for the first time, and afterwards, she asked him his name.

"Yuri," he said. "I just finished Marine boot camp and I'm a freshman at the University of Southern California."

"I haven't seen you here before," she said.

"I'm only here because of my younger brother, David," he said. "Checking the place out." He smiled at her. "You did pretty good in there."

"Thanks," she said.

They chatted a short while until Yuri's brother, David, came out of his group and they left. A few weeks later, he called her at home.

"Hey, remember me? The guy going to USC? The Marine?"

"Yes, I remember," Tara said.

"Listen, I know this is short notice, but I have a Marine Corps Ball coming up in two weeks, and I'd like to take you."

"Well, uh, you'd have to ask my dad," she said.

"Sure, no problem."

"Why don't you come to church on Sunday? You can ask him then."

"Okay, I'll be there."

After church, he found Tara and asked where her dad was.

"Over there," she said, pointing to Jeff, who was shaking hands with people as they left the sanctuary.

"The preacher? He's your dad?"

"That's right." She smiled at him. "You didn't know?"

"No, but it's not a problem." He walked over to Jeff and waited his turn. "Sir, my name is Yuri, and I'm requesting permission to take your daughter to the Marine Corps Ball."

"Really?" Jeff said, eyeing him up and down. He looked over at Tara, who was smiling. "Okay," he said, "I guess that would be all right."

Tara was shocked. She expected a complete interrogation.

Karyn answered the front door when Yuri showed up the night of the ball. There stood this handsome Marine, dressed in his formal white uniform, carrying two-dozen red roses. She invited him in and the minute he stepped inside, Puppers, their dog, growled at him and bit him on the leg. He actually drew blood. "The dog from hell," Yuri thought.

They had a great time together and began dating off and on. Yuri told her he had never dated a white girl before. Only Latinos. He invited her over to meet his parents, who were originally from Ecuador. They were strict Catholics. Tara and Yuri had a number of discussions about what it meant to be a Christian.

"My friend, Angel Cortez, talked to me about Jesus a lot," he said. "He was on the water polo team with me. When the guys would cuss, he'd say, 'My ears aren't trash cans!' Then he'd quote some Bible verse. But me, I'm a good Catholic boy. Once I was even an altar boy." He grinned at Tara, thinking he was impressing her.

She struggled with her feelings towards him, seeing him secretly, knowing her parents didn't approve of her dating someone not fully committed to the Lord. They told her to break it off, and Yuri was furious.

"What?! I'm not good enough?" He reacted when Tara told him. A couple of the guys in the youth group at church told him he should back off, that he wasn't good for the ministry. "They're giving me the boot from church," he thought. "This is incredible." Then he thought one of them was interested in Tara for himself. In spite of all the conflict, they continued to see each other secretly. Then they got sexually involved, and Karyn found out about it.

"This isn't right," she said. "Tara, look at what's happening here. You're messing up your future."

"But he's a good guy," Tara argued. "He's got his whole school and career mapped out; he's very responsible."

"And what about the Lord?" Karyn asked. "His relationship with the Lord is the most important thing."

"He's growing," Tara said defensively.

"Dating is not a mission outreach," Jeff said. "You two need to lighten up."

Tara continued to see Yuri and even accepted an airline ticket he bought so that she could visit him when he was in school in Quantico, Virginia. That did it.

Jeff and Karyn spent many sleepless nights, discussing what to do next. Finally, they told her to stop seeing Yuri or move out. She moved into an apartment with a friend. But she was miserable, guilty, ashamed, and confused. She even had to step down from ministry because of her bad example to the other singles. She started taking sleeping pills because sleep only came in short spurts. One night the turmoil became too much for her, and she overdosed on the pills. When she was discovered, she was rushed to the emergency ward at the hospital. They pumped her stomach.

Karyn and Jeff rushed over there. Karyn tried to hold back the tears as she glared at Yuri. "She hates me," he thought. Jeff took Yuri aside.

"This is obviously not a healthy relationship," he said. "We're going to take Tara home with us. She shouldn't be alone." He sighed, but stayed calm. "Listen Yuri, you guys need to keep it light. It's killing her."

Yuri did feel responsible, yet angry. "I'd like to smack the lightness out of him," he thought. "Doesn't he realize that we love each other?"

Yuri was sent to Japan for over a year and continued to send cards, letters, and gifts. While there, he built a relationship with the chaplain, attending Marine Bible studies and spending time with the chaplain's family. When he came back to the States, Yuri was about to obtain the rank of captain. His goal was to be an instructor of young Marines. He had several conversations with Jeff and Karyn, trying to win their approval, but it didn't work.

"Tara has a call to be in ministry," Karyn said. "And ministry life is different. You can't walk in sin."

Yuri left confused and angry. He finally told Tara, "This whole situation is killing me, you, my family, and your family. I just don't understand it. I can't do this anymore."

They didn't see each other for several months, but then Yuri called and asked her to meet him. He said, "Let's have a nice night together, and then we have to make a decision. Either we go our separate ways, or we get married." He looked at her, fingering the ring he had in his pocket. "Do you want to marry me?"

Tara started crying. "Yes, let's just get married. I know you're a good man, and I love you."

The next day, Yuri drove to the house and asked to speak with Jeff and Karyn.

"I know our relationship has been hard on everyone," Yuri said, "and I appreciate your letting me come here." He was nervous, but confident. "I came to ask for your blessing. Tara and I want to get married."

"No," Jeff said, "You don't have my blessing. You both have to get right before the Lord first."

Tara started crying and dashed out of the room.

"We're getting married," Yuri said. "With or without your blessing."

"You can't do this!" Karyn said.

"Watch me." Yuri stood to his feet. "I came here to tell you we're getting married. I didn't come to ask. If you don't want to give your blessing, that's fine." He marched out of the house.

Several months later, they had a Marine wedding at the base. The night before the wedding, Jeff and Karyn decided they should attend, and Jeff walked Tara down the aisle. He watched as the chaplain performed the ceremony that he had hoped to do himself one day.

On their honeymoon cruise, Tara cried a lot. "This was more like a funeral than a wedding," Yuri thought. When she fell asleep, he went up to the pilothouse. He looked up at the sky. His bride had fallen asleep with a tear-stained face. Tears began to form in his own eyes. "God, what am I supposed to do? What do You want from me?" he said out loud. "Help me figure this out. I know You're real. I want You in my life. Tell me what to do." Tears streamed down his face. He heard a still, small voice within, "Ask for forgiveness." "Okay, forgive me, Lord. I know I messed up, having a sexual relationship before marriage."

"Ask Jeff and Karyn for forgiveness."

"Okay. I will. I want to do things right." He went back to their room with a new peace in his heart.

The day after they got back, Yuri went to Jeff and Karyn and asked for their forgiveness. They talked a long time, discussing all the issues that had been between them, and cleared the air. Their relationship began to blossom as a family. Yuri and Tara held a Bible study at their apartment in San Diego, and some drill instructors came to the Lord.

"What a joy to see the change in Yuri," Jeff said.

Meanwhile, Christy was still seeing Kenny, and they talked about getting married. They decided to go to another

Calvary Chapel where no one knew them. They went through premarital counseling, then told their small group that Christy came from a ministry family and that she already had a child and wanted to get married, but the parents didn't approve. Despite the differences of opinion, they felt led to get married anyway.

Jeff and Karyn were upset and disappointed, but at that point, they knew they had to accept the marriage. Three months later, Christy got pregnant again. Christy named the baby, Natalie, after her sister Linda's birth name. A year later, she had Taryn, a combination of Tara and Karyn.

After a number of months, the Lord did a work in the family's relationship. They came back to Calvary Chapel of Downey, and Jeff and Karyn were blessed to be able to help them purchase their first house.

Linda's marriage was becoming more difficult, with her husband involved in extramarital relationships, drugs, and drinking. Linda had begun taking prescription drugs and was also involved in an extramarital relationship. One day at work, Linda was alone in the chart room at Kaiser where she worked, and the tears started to flow.

"I can't take this anymore, Lord," she said. "Tell me what to do. What?" Suddenly she saw what appeared to be a beam of light in the room. "You need to repent." She sensed God's presence and sobs came from deep within as she poured out her heart, asking for forgiveness. That night she called her adoptive parents and Jeff and Karyn to confess her sins and to restore relationships. She remained with her husband awhile longer, but he continued to go in his own direction, and the marriage ended in divorce.

Just when things seemed to be settling down, Jeff began to feel ill and have bouts with colon infections. Usually antibiotics would get him through it. One Saturday night when Karyn was out of town speaking at a conference, Jeff went to Rusty and Robyn's house for dinner.

"You don't look too good," Robyn said. She put her hand on his forehead. "You've got a fever."

"I'll be okay," he said. But at home, the pain increased, and his abdomen felt hot to the touch. He got through the night and through the Sunday morning church services. Yuri and Tara were there.

"You're in pain," Yuri said. "What's wrong?"

"I don't know," Jeff said, "but it's getting worse."

Yuri drove him to the emergency ward at the hospital, then called Karyn to let her know what was happening. She caught a flight home and Yuri picked her up at the airport. Tara stayed with her dad.

"This is very serious," the doctor said when Karyn arrived. "He has diverticulitis and his large intestine has burst. Peritonitis has set in, so we're going to have to do surgery."

"Just how serious are you talking?" Karyn asked, not sure she really wanted to hear the answer.

"It's possible that he may not make it through surgery," he said somberly.

Karyn started to cry, then began to pray. "Please God, don't take Jeff from me. I need him more than ever. And his work at the church isn't done."

The doctor spoke with Jeff and said, "We're doing surgery and will have to do a colostomy and possibly some skin grafts."

"No," Jeff said. "God is not going to let this happen." He looked up at the doctor. "Are you a Christian?"

"Yes," the doctor said.

"I am too. Let's just pray right now." All Jeff could manage to say was, "In the name of Jesus, heal me." He looked at the doctor and offered a weak smile. "I'm going to be fine."

"Okay, sure." The doctor left the room and the nurses began to prepare Jeff for surgery.

As they wheeled him into the operating room, Jeff stared up at the ceiling grids. "Do you want My will?"

"Yes, Lord, I want Your will."

"Whatever happens, know this. I allowed it."

He came through the surgery, and they left the wound open to heal. The doctor said in a few months they would operate again and try to repair his intestine so he wouldn't have to permanently use a colostomy bag. He had to get others to fill in for him for Sunday services and his other responsibilities. Six weeks later, the doctor successfully performed the second surgery and the colostomy was removed. After being out of the pulpit for four months, Jeff was overjoyed to be back in action. He had new ideas to implement.

Chapter

24

Celebration

One morning when Jeff arrived at his office, Neil approached him.

"Did you see this?" he asked, holding up a newspaper. "The City of Norwalk is canceling their fireworks celebration for the Fourth of July this year. Apparently they're losing money on it in spite of entry fees."

"I think I know what you're about to suggest."

"If we could take over the Cerritos College location for our Freedom Celebration, we would reach a lot more people than we do in our parking lot."

*Jeff inviting people to come to Christ at
the Freedom Celebration, July 4, 2000.*

"We already get a great turnout there for Easter sunrise services, so it makes sense. Check it out," Jeff said. "And by the way, we won't charge an entry fee."

For several years, the church had held a free fireworks display on the Fourth of July in the church parking lot. Thousands came out. First, a band played, then a brief Gospel presentation was given, followed by fireworks. It proved to be a good outreach to the community because many people who would not ordinarily come to a church came to the celebration.

Neil and others got to work and permission was granted to use the stadium for the Fourth of July.

"With what the fire marshal allows, we can seat seventeen thousand people," he reported back to Jeff. "We've rented a stage, hired the sound and light crew, lined up a couple of bands, portable dressing rooms, and the pyrotechnic company is on board. I still need to rent the chairs." He spoke fast and his words tumbled over one another. "I'm getting heart palpitations! This is overwhelming!"

"Trust in the Lord," Jeff said. "I know it's a lot of work, but it will all come together."

On the day of the event, Jeff and Karyn went to the stadium to see how things were coming together and to assist however they could. The place buzzed with activity. Up on the stage, men were doing sound checks. On the field, thousands of chairs were being set up. The pyrotechnic company carefully prepared the fireworks. The team of ushers, counselors, and security personnel were reviewing their areas of responsibility.

Karyn glanced up at the bleachers and noticed someone sitting up there. With matted hair halfway down his back and his ragged clothes, she thought he looked suspicious. She found Neil and asked, "Aren't the doors to the stadium closed until five o'clock tonight? Isn't that when the public is allowed to come in?"

"Yes, that's right," Neil said.

"Well, look up there." She pointed to the bleachers. "There's a street person who's slipped in, and he's sitting up there. You better check him out. If he's drinking or anything, he'll have to leave. He looks pretty scruffy."

"Sure," Neil said. "I'll check it out." He climbed the bleachers and approached the young man. "Hi," Neil said. "How's it going?"

"Great, man," he said. "The sound is great. I think we're ready. It's going to be a great night."

Surprised, Neil held out his hand and said, "I'm Neil Matranga."

"I'm with the band," he said. "Thanks for getting us the dressing rooms." He stood to his feet. "I'd better go get ready. Nice to meet you."

Neil walked back over to Karyn, trying to keep a serious face. "Good thing you told me to check him out," he said.

"How did he slip in?" she asked. "We need to be careful with security."

"He's a band member," Neil said, breaking into a grin. "I told you we got alternative rock 'n' roll bands to reach the kids."

They both laughed. "Whatever it takes," she said.

The stadium filled up quickly once the doors opened. Three bands played for twenty-five minutes each, then Miles McPherson, a former San Diego Charger turned evangelist, gave a brief evangelistic message. People poured out of the stands, coming forward to receive Christ. Staff counselors prayed with each one and gave each a free Bible and study guide. They completed a response card with names and addresses, and these were divided up later among all the pastors and churches who had participated. It was their responsibility to follow up with people from their area. Prior to the event, two hundred letters had been sent out to surrounding churches, inviting their participation. The letter explained that the purpose of the event was to build the Kingdom of God, not to build Calvary Chapel. Counselors and ushers were needed. But only a few churches responded.

The fire marshal required that everyone be back in their seats before the fireworks could begin, so the invitation and follow-up was brief. Over nine hundred came forward. Once everyone was seated again, Jeff stepped onto the stage.

"We're celebrating our independence as a nation tonight, but we're also celebrating our dependence on the Lord. Right? We want to welcome all those who came forward tonight to the family of God!"

The crowd roared their approval. He started the countdown, shouting, "Five, four, three, two, one!"

Suddenly, the fireworks began, and a huge sign lit up that said, "Welcome to the family!" The sky exploded with fireworks for the next twenty minutes. The crowd cheered and clapped. The evening was such a big success that they decided to do it for two nights, the third and Fourth of July, the following year. Three thousand came forward to accept the Lord that weekend.

At the next staff meeting, Neil excitedly reported that one of the couples that worked with the set-up crew had been among those who had come forward. "They were just contracted to bring the stage, and God changed their lives."

Jeff prayed, thanking God for the souls being touched. "We're just hanging on, following You, Lord. Keep showing us what more You want us to do."

Mike Sasso left the meeting thinking, "Wow, Lord, open my eyes so I can see what Jeff sees. He's got such tremendous vision, guts, and faith. If he listened to me, we'd still be playing it safe in a little cracker box on 4th Street!" He marveled at the response from the holiday parades where they built a float and handed out tracts, the alternative activities on Halloween, the Good Friday and Easter services held at the stadium, and now the Freedom Celebrations. Since that first celebration, through speakers including Raul Ries, Mike MacIntosh, Greg Laurie, Jeff Johnson, and others, thousands have come to the Lord every third and Fourth of July.

With so many people responding, baptism services became an event as well. During the winter, they held them at an Olympic-size indoor pool. In the summer, they were held at the beach.

Phil O'Malley went early in the morning with the Senior Saints ministry to Corona del Mar to set up for the baptism service. They put up signs and set up tents for a barbecue. The baptism would be at Pirates Cove on the main beach.

Phil thought back to when he was eight years old and had felt God's presence. He ran to his pastor and told him

Baptism at Pirates Cove, 2000.

he wanted to be baptized. The pastor promised he would do it the following Sunday, so Phil wore the appropriate clothes and brought a towel to dry off afterwards. He could hardly contain his excitement. But when he went up to the pastor, he was told they couldn't do it because another family had priority. The pastor brushed him off. Phil left church that morning crushed. Thirty-five years later, Jeff baptized him at Pirates Cove, along with his wife, son, and daughters.

"Thank You, Lord, that no one will be turned away here," he whispered.

About one thousand people stood along the cliffs around the cove. Several hundred others made their way down to the beach. Loudspeakers were set up in the sand so everyone could hear. Twelve pastors from Calvary Chapel Downey stood at the edge of the water, ready to begin the service.

Baptism at Corona Del Mar, 2001.

People passing by in boats stopped out of curiosity. Some pulled out binoculars to see what was going on.

Jeff walked over to the microphone.

"Your special day is here!" The people standing on the beach and on the cliffs clapped their approval.

He focused his attention on those about to be baptized. "Physically, you're taking a step of faith today. Physically, you're going to feel the water. Emotionally, you're going to experience incredible joy." He looked around at their faces. "There's a special joy in following the Lord in water baptism. So get ready for a blessing as you begin walking over to the water, anticipating what the Lord is going to do

220

as you go down into that watery grave. You see, not only is it physical; not only is it emotional, but it's spiritual.

"It's symbolic of when Jesus went down into the tomb and it was shut up. Likewise, you are going down into the water as a symbol of dying to your old life, then, just as Jesus rose again, so you are going to come out of this water today, walking in the newness of life."

He walked away from the microphone down to the water, wading waist-deep into the ocean. All the pastors followed him, then gathered in a circle, arms linked, and they prayed.

Several hundred people lined up, making their way into the water to be baptized. Those watching began singing choruses, clapping when someone they knew came up out of the water. When they finished, Jeff came out of the water and stepped over to the microphone one more time.

Jeff preaching at a water baptism, 1998.

"Those of you watching may have had a friend or family member baptized today. Maybe you don't fully understand what this is all about. I'm here to tell you, this could be your day. Before I came to the Lord, I was seeking for truth, thinking it was a philosophy. Then I met Jesus, the Son of the living God, and He radically changed my life.

"Could Karl Marx or Sigmund Freud change my life the way it has been changed? Hardly. Marx could give someone a cause, and Freud might say that it's an understanding of one's self. But they couldn't fill that inner void of the soul with love. Love is the greatest miracle, the missing ingredient—a supernatural gift of divine grace from a sovereign God.

"God so loved the world, that to those who receive Him, He gives them power to become the sons of God. If you ask me where this love comes from, I'll say to you, all I know is that once I was blind, but now I see. I was dead, but now I live. Jesus Christ, the Savior of the world, entered into me one day, forgave my sin, and changed me forever. Only God's Messiah can do that.

"My prayer for you is that you will not only get right with God, but that once you turn from your old life to Him, you will be mightily used by Him and you will experience the peace of God." He looked around at the sea of faces. "If this is your day, then come on down. We'll wait for you."

Many more found their way down to the beach and entered the water to be baptized. As Jeff stepped back into the ocean, he thought back to the time he had run through the jungles of Oahu with poison-laced LSD racing through his veins. God took a radical, rebellious drug addict and turned his life right side up. He thought of John 10:10: "The thief comes only in order that he may steal and may kill and may destroy. I (Jesus) came that they may have life, and have it in abundance—to the full, till it overflows."

Tears, not salt water, stung his eyes as he reached toward the first young man to be baptized.

When Calvary Chapel of Downey had a special service on their twenty-fifth anniversary, Pastor Chuck Smith sent a special video to celebrate with them.

"Congratulations for your twenty-five years here in Downey," he said. "Surely the Lord has done exceedingly, abundantly above all that you could have imagined. I remember back in 1973, when I heard that Jeff Johnson had started a Bible study in Downey. We were thrilled at this being one of the first outreaches from Calvary Chapel Costa Mesa.

"I remember being called when the thought came up of getting the old White Front store. It seemed like it was such a huge building at the time. Now look. It's glorious to realize what God has done. But I also know that He's not through yet.

"I have a good friend in ministry who died. He had been in ministry for over fifty years. In the casket, he had a Bible in one hand and a fork in the other. Someone asked 'why?'

"'To represent his ministry,' came the reply. 'He always was a minister of the Word, so the Bible was placed in one hand.'

"'But what about the fork?'

"'Well, he always enjoyed the church potluck dinners. When they collected the plates after dinner, they would say, "keep your fork, the best is yet to come." So there he was in his casket, with the Bible and the fork, because the best was yet to come.' And I believe that is true for you here at Calvary Chapel Downey. The best is yet to come."

Pastor Chuck, Raul Ries, and Jeff at the CC Men's Conference, 2000.

*(Top, l-r) Jon Courson, Jeff, Steve Mays, Greg Laurie, Skip Heitzig
(Bottom) Bil Galatin, Pastor Chuck, and Don McClure, 1991.*

*Mike MacIntosh, Jeff, and Greg Laurie
at the Jesus People Reunion, 1999.*

Epilogue

Jeff Johnson's story is not over. New chapters are being written daily.

He and Karyn are happy to be in a good relationship with each of their children. **Jeffrey** graduated from UC Santa Cruz with a B.A. in psychology. He currently lives and works in San Francisco.

Karyn, Jeff, Gary, & Carolyn (Linda's adoptive parents) in Israel, 1992.

After being a single mom for several years, **Linda** married Jay, a Christian man who is the landscape maintenance supervisor for the church and school property. Linda took an administrative management position at Calvary Chapel Christian School, where her two children, Jason and Emily, attend. Linda's adoptive parents have gone on several Israel trips with Jeff and Karyn, and they have spent several holidays together as a family.

Christy and Kenny have three children: Laura, Natalie, and Taryn. They attend Calvary Chapel Downey. Their children attend the Calvary Chapel Christian School. Christy is a full-time mom.

Tara and Yuri have three children, Andrew, Abigail, and Annie Jo. Yuri left the Marines, then became a Beverly Hills police officer. He began to feel the call toward ministry, and when a position at the school became available, he left the police force and began working as an administrator at the school. He also works with the *Shields of Faith* ministry.

The grandkids: Emily, Abigail, Natalie, Taryn, Andrew, Jason, and Laura, 2001. (Note: When this photo was taken, Annie Jo had not yet been born.)

On one of their trips to Israel, Jeff had the privilege of performing a wedding ceremony on the shores of the Sea of Galilee where Yuri and Tara renewed their vows. Tara is a full-time mom and is active with the women's ministry and worship team at church.

The Fellowship

The church has an attendance of approximately nine thousand, and the Christian school has twelve hundred students. Another building program is underway to add on to the current structure in order to provide more office space for the pastors and for counseling.

Other Calvary Chapels that have been birthed through Jeff Johnson's ministry include ten in California, five in Russia, one each in Peru, Mexico, Africa, and Colorado. Who knows what God has planned for the future? To God be the glory!

Calvary Chapel Downey Ministries Include:

Missions: More than seventy missionaries were sent out from the church in 2002. Long-term missionaries are stationed in Russia, the Philippines, Africa, Peru, and Mexico. Short-term involvement included teams sent to Russia, France, Uganda, the Philippines, Morocco, Yucatan, Ireland, China, Sudan, Hopi Indian Reservation in Arizona, and our Kid's Kingdom orphanage in Mexico. Financial support is also given to Operation Mobilization, YWAM, Child Evangelism, and the *Calvary Chapel Magazine*. Regular missions prayer meetings are held at the church as is a missions training class.

Evangelism: Outreach includes concerts, school campus activities, Easter Celebrations at Cerritos stadium, "*Sound Doctrine*" radio ministry, Fourth of July Freedom Celebration, summer Harvest Crusades, street witnessing, a cult ministry (*Ready Defense*), and the Downey Christmas Parade.

Youth Ministry: Weekly study groups are provided for teenagers. There are also special outings, discipleship groups, and a complete summer program, including everything from summer camps to missions trips.

Children's Ministry: From infants up to sixth grade, activities include Bible lessons, Vacation Bible School (one thousand kids each summer), Special Kids (handicapped), Children's Prayer Chain, "Straight Up" puppet ministry, "Glad Scientist," Pioneer Clubs (boys and girls club setting), camps, summer outreach trips, and new believer correspondence.

Calvary Chapel Christian School: Provides Christian education for twelve hundred students from kindergarten through twelfth grade. There is also an independent study program providing professional guidance to parents who wish to educate their children at home.

Social Ministries: *House of Ruth* adoption services provides ministry to women in crisis pregnancies. *New Life Prison Ministry* reaches out to those in prison and to their families, provides a chaplain's program that reaches into prisons throughout California, holds prison conferences and training for volunteers, has established both the *House of Jeremiah* (for men coming out of prison) and the *House of Esther* (for women). The *Convalescent Outreach* ministers to those in local convalescent homes. *Crossroads* is a pro-life ministry, including post abortion support groups, and *Women 4 Women*. Advancing Christian Traditions in Our Nation (*A.C.T.I.O.N.*) keeps the church body apprised of governmental and moral issues affecting our world.

Church Ministries: Pastoral and Biblical guidance is available through spiritual, emotional, premarital, and marital counseling. Men's ministries include a weekly Saturday morning prayer meeting, *Man to Man*, a weekly Bible study, men's retreats, and special events throughout the year. Women's ministries include a weekly Bible study, Friday morning prayer, prayer chain, women's retreats, Victorious Overcomers in Christ Everyday (*V.O.I.C.E.*) for abused women, and *Firm Believers' Women's Aerobics*.

Weekly worship services and Bible studies are held for the Spanish and Arabic communities.

New Hope Addiction Ministry is for individuals and families dealing with substance abuse as well as other addictions. *Helps Committee* provides food for funerals, food for the needy, and various other helps as needed. Home Bible studies are held weekly, and *Essentials of Christianity* classes are taught which include providing spiritual service training. Fellowship involvement includes *Senior Saints, Celebrating Marriage, College & Career*, Tuesday morning Bible study, Believers' Meeting, Ushers, Singles' Fellowship, Single Parents, all-church picnics, all-church camp outs, and *Surfers for Christ*.

Calvary Chapel Bible College Downey provides a Bachelor's Degree in Biblical Studies, an Associates Degree in Theology, and a Certificate of Completion (for those who have not graduated from high school). The *Chapel Store* offers a selection of Christian literature and gift items. The *Chapel Café* serves a variety of foods and drinks, along with music and entertainment from musical groups within the church. There's a Video & Lighting ministry, and the Music ministry includes worship teams for Sunday services and other events. They have produced a number of worship albums that have blessed the body of Christ.

Calvary Chapel Downey today.
"The Best is Yet to Come!"

The Seeker's Prayer

If you want a personal relationship with God and the assurance that your sins have been forgiven, here is a suggested prayer ...

Father, I come to You, confessing my sin and asking for Your forgiveness. I thank You, Lord, for You have promised that if I will confess my sins, You will be faithful to forgive me and cleanse me from all unrighteousness. I want to turn from my sins and live in a way that will please You. I ask for Your help, Lord. I ask that You give me the power through Your Holy Spirit to live the right way.

I thank You that Jesus Christ died on the cross, paying the price for my sins, and then rose from the dead. I accept Him now as my Savior, my Lord, and my friend.

I also thank You because You have said that whoever comes to You, You will in no wise cast out. Thank You for giving me a new life in Christ. I surrender myself to You. Make me what You want me to be. In Jesus' Name. Amen.

What Next?

If you have decided to accept Jesus Christ as your Savior, you are now born again (John 1:12). Here are a few things that will help you to grow as a Christian:

1. PRAY—Prayer is like a telephone line that goes directly to God. It's important to spend time talking to Him every day, the more time the better. Philippians 4:6

2. READ THE BIBLE—The Bible is like a love letter from God. The more you read it, the more you'll fall in love with Him. I Peter 2:2

3. FELLOWSHIP—You need to have friends who share your beliefs and who encourage you. This is why it is so important to find a good, Bible-believing church where you can meet other Christians. Hebrews 10:24-25

4. WITNESS TO OTHERS—Share your faith in Jesus Christ with others. Pray that the Lord will reveal how you should witness and when. Mark 16:15[9]

Contact Information

If you have prayed to receive Christ and to experience God's love and forgiveness, we would love to talk with you and give you a Bible and a Bible study. We want you to know God's love and His plan for your life. Please contact us through our website or at our church office:

Calvary Chapel of Downey
12808 Woodruff Avenue
Downey, CA 90242
562.803.5631
calvarychapel.org/downey

Endnotes

1. Paramahansa Yogananda. *WHERE THERE IS LIGHT: Insight & Inspiration for Meeting Life's Challenges.* <http://www.yogananda-srf.org/writings/love_main.html>, (February 6, 2003).

2. Demonically-inspired out-of-body experiences.

3. Jeff was obviously hallucinating at this point; however, the waves were very large on this particular day due to the weather.

4. Author unknown, "Christian House-McCahill Studied," *The Call-Enterprise,* date and page unknown.

5. Robert Burns, "Storefront church is Downey's largest," *Southeast News,* February 8, 1990, p. B-1.

6. Ibid.

7. Close-up section, "Pastor serves as Downey's first police chaplain," *Press-Telegram,* March 15, 1989, p. B-3.

8. Bob Houser, "Calvary Chapel converts White Front to religion," *Press-Telegram,* December 3, 1990, pgs. C-1 and C-4.

9. "The Seeker's Prayer" and "What Next?" adapted from *How Can a Man be Born Again?* by Pastor Chuck Smith. © 2002 by The Word For Today by permission of The Word For Today, P.O. Box 8000, Costa Mesa, California, 92628.